I. M. Pei

ARCHITECT OF TIME, PLACE, AND PURPOSE
BY JILL RUBALCABA

I.M.Pei

ARCHITECT OF TIME, PLACE, AND PURPOSE
BY JILL RUBALCABA

MARSHALL CAVENDISH

For Dan—Always

Other Marshall Cavendish Offices: Marshall Cavendish International (Asia) Private Limited, 1 New Industrial Road, Singapore 536196 • Marshall Cavendish International (Thailand) Co Ltd. 253 Asoke, 12th Flr, Sukhumvit 21 Road, Klongtoey Nua, Wattana, Bangkok 10110, Thailand • Marshall Cavendish (Malaysia) Sdn Bhd, Times Subang, Lot 46, Subang Hi-Tech Industrial Park, Batu Tiga, 40000 Shah Alam, Selangor Darul Ehsan, Malaysia

Marshall Cavendish is a trademark of Times Publishing Limited

Rubalcaba, Jill.
I.M. Pei : architect of time, place, and purpose / by Jill Rubalcaba. — 1st ed.
p. cm.
Includes bibliographical references.
ISBN 978-0-7614-5973-6 (hardcover) – ISBN 978-0-7614-6081-7 (ebook) 1. Pei, I. M., 1917–Juvenile literature. 2. Chinese American architects–Biography–Juvenile literature. I. Pei, I. M., 1917- II. Title. III. Title: Architect of time, place, and purpose.

NA737.P365R83 2011   2011001910
720.92—dc22
[B]

Book design by Alex Ferrari
Editor: Margery Cuyler

Printed in China
First edition
10 9 8 7 6 5 4 3 2 1

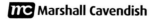 Marshall Cavendish

Acknowledgments

When I first discovered that the responsibility for acquiring images for this book would be mine, I was filled with dread. For a brief moment, I considered scrapping the project entirely. What did I know about navigating digital archives in search of the perfect photograph? It was my great fortune that the first person I contacted was Yvonne Mondragon at the National Center for Atmospheric Research in Boulder, Colorado. After our very first phone conversation, my dread evaporated and instead I found myself looking forward to the contacts I would make hunting down these images. Several phone conversations and dozens of emails later, I began to feel a true connection to the vitality of Mr. Pei's building in Boulder—and to Yvonne as well. I think if we lived closer to one another, we would become good friends.

Buoyed by my experience with Yvonne, I contacted the Miho Museum in Kyoto. There, despite my complete ignorance of Japanese, the gracious Akiko Nambu provided hauntingly beautiful images of the bell tower and the museum. Thank you, Akiko Nambu. I look forward to expressing my gratitude in person one day.

At the John F. Kennedy Library, a team of archivists enthusiastically suggested many possible images, making the greatest challenge choosing. Thank you Nadia Dixon, Sharon Kelly, Ethan Hawkley, and Laurie Austin. Also, thanks to Jean Henry at the National Gallery of Art who answered my many beginner's questions and searched the National Gallery's extensive library.

I was beginning to think that this image procurement business wasn't so bad after all. Each contact taught me something unexpected. I was learning firsthand about one of Mr. Pei's principal visions—how people used his buildings. I was sure it couldn't get any better. That's when I met Emma Cobb at Pei Cobb Freed & Partners. As you can see by the number of images credited to Pei Cobb Freed & Partners, Emma worked tirelessly selecting the best possible images that would complement the text and appeal to readers. She answered endless emails and no matter how trivial the question, she never made me feel as though I were pestering her, although surely I was. I am in debt to Emma for enlarging this story, maintaining good spirits through it all, and, of course, supplying these incredible images.

I would like to thank Mr. Pei's personal assistant, Nancy Robinson, for giving generously of her time in reading this manuscript, becoming an invaluable resource, and helping ensure accuracy.

I think the expression "it takes a village" applies to the book-making business. Where would I be without Margery Cuyler's enthusiasm for the project and creative guidance throughout? She took a skeleton and added the flesh. Thank you, Margery. Thanks, too, to Michelle Andreani for herding the cats. Deborah Parker lent the careful eye it takes to copyedit. And the book's design is the brilliant work of Art Director Anahid Hamparian and designer Alex Ferrari. As always I am grateful to my agent, Ginger Knowlton, for handling all things business related. It's freeing to know that aspect of every project is in such capable hands.

My writer's group keeps me sane, ups my game, and makes this job fun. Thank you Jenny Lecce, Molly Lazear Turner, and Jean Ann Wertz. And especially to Dan, without whom I wouldn't get to do this. Thank you.

Photo Credits

The photographs in this book are used by permission and by courtesy of:

CONTENTS

IN THIS TRADITIONAL CHINESE GARDEN IN MODERN-DAY SUZHOU, SHADED PAVILIONS AND PONDS OFFER PLACES TO MEDITATE AND CONNECT WITH NATURE.

The Early Years

It was the Year of the Snake. Snake years are tumultuous times. Restless, squabbling, clashing, sometimes even breaking-out-into-war times. So it was in 1917 China, the Year of the Fire Snake—the most volatile and vicious snake of them all.

It was the Warlord Era. Province pitted against province. The Chinese in the north against the Chinese in the south. Bridges bombed. Homes destroyed. Generational gardens razed to ruin.

With farms torched to blackened wasteland, food grew scarce. Peasants chewed tree bark to ease the ache of empty stomachs. Desperate parents traded their children for bags of rice. Fresh burial mounds swelled across cemeteries—so many of them they looked like waves on a choppy sea.

On the eastern border of China, in Suzhou, one of China's oldest and most beautiful cities, one man worked day and night to save the city from destruction. Li-tai Pei negotiated with warlords. Bribed generals. Pleaded with soldiers. Argued with officers. All to save his ancient city. Amid the mayhem Li-tai Pei's grandson, Ieoh Ming Pei, was born.

He came into the world in that Year of the Snake. Chinese astrologists claim that children born in the Year of the Snake are determined. They excel at solving complex puzzles and can be depended on to overcome even the most difficult obstacles. Snake-born children plan carefully. And in their careers they reach soaring heights. In war-torn China, the snake-child first must survive. Many did not. Bloated corpses, disfigured from starvation, littered the streets.

Ieoh Ming Pei's grandfather grew weaker and weaker from the exhausting bargaining. He managed to save Suzhou's roads, schools, orphanages, and hospitals, but he could not save his son and his son's family. Unlike his father, Tsuyee Pei refused to negotiate with the militia. Orders were issued for the family's arrest.

Disguised as a Western woman, Tsuyee led his wife and two children along the canals of Suzhou, over the cobblestone streets, and through a maze of squat, whitewashed homes with gray tile roofs. Ieoh Ming clung to his nursemaid's back with one hand while reaching for the laundry that fluttered from long poles with the other. Ieoh Ming was too young to understand the dangers in this escape to Hong Kong, too young to know the word *war*. Too young to be afraid.

The island of Hong Kong, ruled by Great Britain for decades, bustled with foreigners. The British loved their tea, and dockside warehouses were bursting with it. Merchants displayed silks and cotton. Traders offered porcelain and lacquerware. For a banker like Tsuyee Pei, who knew the financial ways of the West, Hong Kong was the place to succeed. It wasn't long before the Bank of China awarded Tsuyee Pei a bank manager's position in their Shanghai branch.

The family of ten-year-old Ieoh Ming Pei had grown. In addition to his older sister, Yuen Hua, he now had a younger sister, Wei, and two brothers, Yu Kun and Yu Tsung. All five children walked wide-eyed through the streets of Shanghai. Ford Model Ts, their horns sounding an impatient *aaaooogah*, barreled down on bare-foot coolies pulling rickshaws. Gussied-up Parisian ladies in satin gowns brandished foot-long cigarette holders and sashayed past Russian panhandlers. Turbaned Sikh traffic officers with jangling steel bracelets waved along European pedestrians. In Hong Kong, the Peis had been exposed to the world outside of China, but nothing had prepared them for this kaleidoscope of cultures in Shanghai.

Ieoh Ming Pei remembers, "It was a very exciting, but also a corrupt place. So I learned both good and bad from Shanghai."

As Ieoh Ming's father became more and more successful, he had less and less time for his children—not that his father ever was the type to "pat a son on the back, or hug a daughter," Ieoh Ming recalls. Although Ieoh Ming Pei was never close to his distant father, the memory of his mother—eighty years later—still has the power to bring him to tears.

Ieoh Ming remembers listening to her play the flute, laugh with friends, and recite her poems. Twice she brought Ieoh Ming with her on meditation retreats to a Buddhist monastery high in the mountains. It was hard for a young boy to sit still and be quiet hour after hour, with no playmates and nothing to do.

At night the silence was so thick and deep Ieoh Ming would strain to hear a sound—any sound.

Kneeling.

Motionless.

Waiting.

For the plop of a raindrop. The chirp of a cricket. The rustle of a tree branch. But he heard nothing, nothing at all.

"Then, just before dawn," Ieoh Ming said, "there was a strange creaking, groaning sound. It was the shoots of young bamboo, all coming up from the earth at the same time. This was the great gift my mother had given me—to hear the silence."

During the school year, Ieoh Ming and his classmates from the Protestant missionary school spent their weekends going to movies and playing billiards. On his way to the Midtown cinema and pool hall, Ieoh Ming passed the Park Hotel. "This building was going up, getting taller and taller," Ieoh Ming said. "At the time it was my favorite building. It was the tallest building in the Far East." With each floor, Ieoh Ming's fascination grew. Before the building was finished, Ieoh Ming knew what he wanted to do with his life—design buildings.

When Ieoh Ming was only thirteen, his mother died of cancer and his father, depressed, traveled to Europe to grieve, leaving his children to find their own way through their sadness. Ieoh Ming, who had been close to his mother, felt forlorn. Being the oldest son, he was supposed to help his brothers and sisters, but how could he do that when he wasn't sure how to manage his own sorrow?

Tsuyee Pei arrived back in China with a much younger woman. The woman had agreed to marry Tsuyee—if, and only if, the children lived somewhere else. Ieoh Ming's father rented an apartment, hired a housekeeper, and shooed off his children. Still reeling from the loss of their mother, they now could not even find comfort in their family home.

Fifty miles from Shanghai, in Suzhou, Ieoh Ming's grandfather made plans. He worried that Ieoh Ming's education was unbalanced with so much exposure to modern ways. Shanghai was no place to learn traditional Chinese values. Meditating on the chrysanthemums that filled his courtyards, Ieoh Ming's grandfather prepared to bring his grandchildren to the ancestral home, where he would teach Ieoh Ming Confucian ethics. He must learn the importance of humanity, integrity, and righteousness, the worth of loyalty, piety, and kindness. The boy must know his place in the long line of ancestors. Li-tai Pei would see to it.

The road from Shanghai to Suzhou was flat and dusty, carving its way through treeless farmland. With each passing mile, Ieoh Ming felt as if he were journeying back in time. Centuries melted away. And when Ieoh Ming finally reached the walled city of Suzhou, and passed through the town gates, it was as if the modern world no longer existed. Confucius and Buddha would have felt at home in Suzhou's temples, pagodas, and gardens. There is a Chinese proverb: In heaven there is paradise, on earth there is Suzhou.

Mandarins, the wealthy, and the powerful, retreated to Suzhou to reflect. In Suzhou, Confucian virtues were a way of life—a way of being and behaving in the physical world to achieve social harmony.

Ieoh Ming Pei spent his summers exploring the Garden of the Lion Forest, the Pei family retreat. Chinese gardens are designed to give the illusion of the natural world. Footbridges hump in cat-stretch arcs suggesting mountains. Meandering pebble paths switch back like rivers, leading deeper into the garden. "You see a bit," Ieoh Ming explains, "then you are led on. You never see the whole thing."

Lion Forest's many vistas had names. The Peis, dressed in long silk gowns with broad mandarin sleeves, might read poetry in Sleeping Cloud Room, or meditate on plum blossoms in the Place Where One Questions the Plum Tree. The garden spot, Standing in the Snow Reading, got its name when a student waited patiently through a snowstorm for his napping tutor to wake up. Ieoh Ming and his cousins played hide-and-seek in the garden rooms while the elders practiced calligraphy and studied Chinese classics.

No feature in a Chinese garden is accidental, and nothing illustrates this better than the rocks in the Lion Forest. Each porous volcanic rock was selected by a rock farmer for the spirit he saw within the rock. He then carefully chiseled openings, preparing the rock for planting. Once the rock farmer was satisfied, he planted the rock near the edge of a stream or lake where currents smoothed and shaped the stone even more. This shaping might take decades—even centuries. The rock farmer's great-grandson might be the one who would finally

AS A CHILD, IEOH MING PLAYED ALONG THE WINDING PATHS OF LION GROVE GARDEN IN SUZHOU.
THE GARDEN GOT ITS NAME FROM THE ROCKS SHAPED LIKE ROARING LIONS.

harvest what the rock farmer had sown. This patience that goes beyond one lifetime, this continuity through the generations—this connection—is what Ieoh Ming's grandfather hoped to teach his grandchildren.

It wasn't until much later that Ieoh Ming realized how his work had been affected by the ancestral gardens. He likened his buildings to the rock sculptures. "Their shapes have hopefully been chosen most carefully, placed most carefully to respond to the functional currents swirling around them."

Pei Comes to the United States

August 1935

In the early 1900s it was common for Chinese of privilege to attend college in Europe and the United States. Ieoh Ming Pei spent many hours in the library thumbing through college catalogues. After much deliberation, he decided on the University of Pennsylvania. The descriptions of the courses about architecture captured his interest.

But after moving to the United States and spending only two weeks at the university, Pei began to doubt his choice. To study architecture in America in 1935 meant mastering the Beaux-Arts style, often by sketching all the flourishes and classic elements from ancient buildings in Greece and Rome. Pei was not interested in becoming a draftsman—merely copying designs from the past. His strengths were math and science, not drawing. Pei transferred to MIT to study engineering.

The dean of architecture at MIT, William Emerson, essayist and lecturer Ralph Waldo Emerson's great-nephew, recognized Pei's gift for design and set out to lure Pei away from engineering. He invited Pei to his house

CLASSIC ELEMENTS IN PERFECT SYMMETRY ARE TYPICAL OF THE BEAUX-ARTS STYLE PRESENT IN THE COLUMNS, BALUSTRADES, ARCHED WINDOWS, AND DOORWAYS OF THE FRENCH ART MUSEUM PALAIS DES BEAUX-ARTS DE LILLE.

for Thanksgiving dinner. When Emerson tried to persuade Pei to transfer into architecture, Pei argued that he was not much of a draftsman and never would be. In the end Emerson convinced Pei to give architecture another try.

Pei and his classmates doggedly worked at their drafting tables copying again and again Beaux-Arts balustrades and columns, arched windows and pedimented doors. They mastered the style and symmetry, but longed for something else. Something new. Something inspiring. The impetus came from an unexpected source—the Depression. Suddenly, grand and opulent seemed excessive and inappropriate. "I was not satisfied with the Beaux-Arts training, nor were many of my contemporaries," Pei said. "So we began to look elsewhere for inspiration. The library was a main source. It was at the library that I learned about Le Corbusier."

Le Corbusier—previously known as Charles-Édouard Jeanneret the painter—changed his name, and with it his profession. As an architect Le Corbusier, or Corbu, as the students at MIT called him, was every bit as avant-garde as he had been as a painter. Born in Switzerland, he became a French citizen in his thirties and advocated many of the modern ideas coming out of Europe.

Scrap history, junk the past—embrace the new. Corbu's modernism demanded a novel way of looking at how humans interacted with architecture. He called for purity of form. Corbu's vision of simple, functional construction embracing new technologies sparked controversy among the Beaux-Arts diehards. But the MIT students, parched for something different, were drawn to his radical ideas. He spoke of houses designed like "machines for living" and described the fussiness of Beaux-Arts as necessary as "a feather is on a woman's head." The students couldn't get enough.

In MIT's libraries, Pei devoured Corbu's books. The essays influenced his early years. "Le Corbusier's three books were my bible. They were the only thing I could rely on to see anything new in architecture. I cannot forget Le Corbusier's visit to MIT in November 1935, dressed in black, with his thick glasses." During his American tour of museums and universities, the irreverent Corbu ridiculed the current state of architecture. He called the skyscrapers of New York City "romantic" but claimed that they had come at a price: "the street has been killed and the city made into a mad-house."

No tedious, detailed renderings of fluted columns for Corbu. With colored pastels, on giant sheets of white paper tacked to the back wall, Corbu scribbled with the same intensity with which he lectured. "I take great pleasure in making large, ten-foot, colored frescoes which become the striking stenographic means, enlivened by red, green, brown, yellow, black, or blue, for expressing . . . my ideas about the reorganization of daily life," Corbu wrote.

His audience at MIT was as spellbound with Corbu's delivery as they were enthralled with his revolutionary philosophies on modern architecture and urban development. Pei said, "He was insolent. He was abusive . . . we had to be shocked out of our complacency." And yet, many members of the American architectural community were not ready for such sweeping change.

ARCHITECT LE CORBUSIER, OR CORBU, AS HIS MIT STUDENTS AFFECTIONATELY CALLED HIM (LEFT), JOINS HARVARD CHAIRMAN AND ARCHITECT WALTER GROPIUS AT AN EXHIBITION IN BERLIN. BOTH WERE PASSIONATE ADVOCATES OF MODERN DESIGN.

Corbu left the United States with no commissions. On his return to France he wrote *When the Cathedrals Were White: Journey to the Country of Timid People*, criticizing Americans for lacking courage and vision. But for Pei, those two days spent watching Corbu's passionate lectures on modernism "were probably the most important days in my architectural education."

During the school year, Pei drove to Grand Central Station in New York City to pick up a fraternity brother who was traveling by train from the West Coast. When his friend got off the train, he introduced Pei to a woman acquaintance, Eileen Loo. Loo was on her way to Wellesley College. While Loo waited for her connecting train, Pei tried to convince her to let him drive her to Boston. He was smitten.

Loo refused, but when Pei discovered that her train had been delayed in Hartford because of a hurricane, Pei called her and teased that she should have taken him up on his offer. Then he asked her out. It was the beginning of a determined and ultimately successful courtship. Five days after Loo's graduation they were married.

The young couple was eager to return to China, but the Japanese had invaded their homeland and Pei's father warned them that it was not safe. They had to wait.

Pei accepted a job in Boston, and Eileen enrolled in Harvard's Graduate School of Design to study landscape architecture. Listening to his wife and her school friends discuss their classes, Pei became intrigued with Harvard's progressive approach to architecture. Harvard's dean of architecture, Joseph Hudnut, had long since shifted his focus from the Gothic style to the modernist. A vocal advocate of this revolution in design, he stunned American architects by appointing a new chairman, Walter Gropius.

In Germany, Gropius had founded a school of architecture called Bauhaus, which means "house of building" in German. His revolutionary philosophy called for artists and architects to work together, joining art with technology in design. Hudnut was excited by the idea of integrating all of the arts into architecture to make it functional as well as visually appealing. However, the Nazis in Gropius's homeland had a different viewpoint. They saw Gropius's vision and the Bauhaus school's teachings as an expression of socialism contaminating the Fatherland. Harassed by the Nazis, Gropius fled to England and then to the United States, where he accepted the position at Harvard.

In the winter of 1942, Pei enrolled in a master's program at Harvard. But it was wartime. And not long after he began his studies, Pei took a leave of absence to help with the war effort. Instead of planning new ways to construct buildings, Pei was assigned the task of finding new ways to destroy them. "It was awful," Pei said. "I don't even like to think about it."

When the war ended, Pei returned to Harvard with Eileen and their new son, T'ing Chung. They had considered moving home to China, but in 1945 China was still in turmoil and Pei's father once again warned the young couple against returning to a country plagued by civil war.

Under Gropius's leadership, Harvard's school of architecture had undergone radical changes during the war. Gropius had removed art history from the core curriculum. In fact, the entire educational direction had taken an anti-historical turn. Gropius went so far as to forbid plaster casts of classical sculpture in the classroom buildings. He justified such radical extremes by saying, "If the college is to be the cultural breeding ground for the coming generation, its attitude should be creative, not imitative. . . . For how can we expect our youngsters to become bold and fearless in thought and action if we encase them timidly in sentimental shrines feigning a culture which has long since disappeared?"

Although Pei admired Gropius as a great teacher, he could not bring himself to agree with Gropius that history had no place in architecture. Perhaps society had outgrown the ornamentation of the Beaux-Arts style, but history could still surface and reveal itself through the spirit of the design. "I wouldn't say he was a great artistic influence in the architectural sense," Pei said, and yet he did feel indebted to Gropius for teaching him method. "Look for logic," Pei explained. "There must be an answer for something—it cannot be just whimsical."

After Pei graduated, once again the Peis felt the tug of their homeland. And once again strife and turmoil prevented their return. Pei remembers, "I wanted to go home. Yet I knew it would not be right to go back at that time. Teaching was the only thing I could do, because I couldn't go in and say to someone, 'I'm going to work for you, but I may leave six months from now.' In teaching you can." The Peis waited some more.

Six months turned into a year. And the Peis had a second son, Chien Chung, ("Didi"). They didn't bother to teach their children Chinese, since they thought the children would pick it up much faster in China when they all returned home. One year turned into two. Americans had taken to calling Ieoh Ming, I. M., which was easier for the American tongue than the Chinese name Ieoh Ming. The months ticked by. The seasons passed. And Pei realized it was time to stop waiting. It was time to practice architecture, not just talk about it.

House Architect
1948 - 1960

If you close your eyes and imagine a cartoon wheeler-dealer real estate tycoon, you probably will come close to a picture of William Zeckendorf. With a phone in one hand and a fat cigar in the other, Zeckendorf conducted big business. Around the time I. M. Pei and Zeckendorf met, Zeckendorf was trying to persuade the United Nations to move their headquarters to New York City. Zeckendorf had purchased 14 blocks of slaughterhouses and slums on the East Side. He had planned to bulldoze the whole lot and build skyscraper hotels and office buildings, but instead he offered the site to the United Nations—and they could name the price. Eight days after he made the offer, he closed the deal.

It's a wonder that when Pei first walked into Zeckendorf's office in the spring of 1948, he didn't turn around and walk right back out. Stained curtains, a threadbare sofa reeking of stale cigar smoke, and "artwork" that consisted of photographs of parking garages would have repelled someone far less meticulous than I. M. Pei. "The whole environment was seedy. It was clear that we were complete opposites," Pei recalls.

They were opposites in demeanor as well. Zeckendorf was as loud and boisterous and boorish as Pei was quiet and reserved and refined. It seems there is truth to the saying that opposites attract. The two took an immediate liking to one another. And when Zeckendorf discovered that both he and Pei had been born in the Year of the Snake, he decided that the fates had thrown them together. Zeckendorf offered Pei a job as his in-house architect. Together, Zeckendorf told Pei, they would redesign the cities of North America. Pei accepted. "I wanted to learn something about real estate. But to my surprise I learned a lot from this man." Among other things, Pei said, "I learned a lot about the politics of building." Zeckendorf's grand plan was to wipe out inner city slums and rebuild. Pei explained their mission, "What was important was creating livable housing at the lowest possible cost, with the highest possible architectural and planning standards."

Triggered by this examination of what makes a home and how one lives in it, I. M. and Eileen began to reflect on their own lives. It was becoming clear that China was no longer the same place that dwelled in their hearts. It was not easy to let go of their dream of one day returning home. They had, as they described it, "Feelings of sorrow at having to abandon our culture, our roots, our ancestral home." And yet, they understood in the postwar communist People's Republic of China, Pei would not have the freedom to fully express himself through his designs. And for that freedom of artistic expression, he felt gratitude to his adopted country. "America has been a blessing to me. It has given me a dimension of challenge which I don't think I would have been able to experience anywhere else." On November 11, 1955, Eileen and I. M. stood with 10,000 other immigrants in New York City's Polo Grounds and took the oath of American citizenship.

Zeckendorf did everything in a big way. He had a nose for finding projects—big projects. He took on the major cities of North America, and like everything else he did, he attacked the challenge with gusto. Zeckendorf purchased a DC-3 for reconnaissance. He and Pei circled target cities and examined prospective sites from the air. Then Zeckendorf hit the ground running. First, a press conference to boost local support. Next, meetings with bankers and politicians. Finally, a tour of the site with Pei. While Zeckendorf razzle-dazzled city officials, Pei spoke with merchants and residents, assessing how people used their part of the city.

For their first major project together, Zeckendorf and Pei chose the city of Denver. In 1950, Denver was suffering like many other American cities. Veterans returning from World War II were guaranteed home loans with the GI Bill. Some 2.4 million took advantage of this benefit and bought homes in the suburbs, deserting the inner cities. Pei envisioned a multi-use center that would lure people back into the city. His strategy was to create a parklike environment using just a fraction of the available land for building. When he proposed his plan to

Zeckendorf—setting the building back and its footprint only taking up a quarter of the two-acre site—Zeckendorf balked. All that empty space which could bring in income seemed wasteful to the real estate developer. In defense, Pei quoted the Chinese philosopher Lao-tzu, "The essence of a vessel is in its emptiness."

The empty space for gardens and fountains wasn't the only unconventional idea in Pei's plan. He wanted the building to be visually appealing, calming, and restorative. First-floor shops with their cluttered window displays were anything but. The problem was that those shops brought in revenue, which was why most multi-use buildings positioned their stores at street level. "They will cheapen the building," Pei argued. "By adding just five cents to the rental of each square foot of space in those twenty-three floors, you will more than make up for the loss of revenue on the ground floor. And because this will be such a beautiful building, you will be able to get your premium rent."

In the end Pei got his way. Pei remarks about Zeckendorf, "He was very open minded, he was. He said let's try. And at the time I think it was rather unusual for a businessman to waste real estate." But it turned out this real estate was anything but a waste. The Mile High Center, named after the city's nickname, with its refrigerated pool stocked with Colorado trout, heated (in the winter) patterned pavement, gardens, trees shading benches, illuminated fountains, and strains of music playing until midnight did attract people—by the droves. Zeckendorf was able to charge twice the going rate for rents, and he still had the lowest vacancy rate of any building in the city. Mile High Center, Denver's first skyscraper, was a smashing success.

One success followed another. Business was good. It wasn't long before Pei could no longer handle all the work himself and had to hire more architects. Pei needed two secretaries, one whose sole job was to manage Pei's complicated schedule. And things were no less busy at home. Pei's family was growing. In 1950 Eileen

WILLIAM ZECKENDORF LISTENS TO I. M. PEI SPEAK. THE TWO COLLABORATED FOR A DECADE ON BUILDING AFFORDABLE HOUSING WITHOUT SACRIFICING EXCELLENT DESIGN.

DENVER'S FIRST SKYSCRAPER, THE MILE HIGH CENTER, HAS THE UNUSUAL FEATURE OF A PARK-LIKE GROUND LEVEL WITH PATTERNED PAVEMENT, TREES, AND SHADED AREAS FOR VISITORS' ENJOYMENT.

gave birth to their third son, Li Chung ("Sandi"). Eileen remembers those hectic days. "He needed eight hours of sleep, but he often got only six. I would get up to go to the bathroom and find little pieces of paper all over the apartment reminding him to try this or that, or get in touch with someone."

With the mounting pressures that come with success, the Peis decided they needed a retreat—a place to enjoy friends and family away from hectic business demands. They found just the spot on a hilltop thirty miles northeast of the city, in the rural town of Katonah, New York, in Westchester County. "I had very little money in those days, but just because your budget is limited doesn't mean you can't build. It just means you do something different," Pei said. To keep labor costs down, Pei used prefabricated sections and arranged them as they are in Chinese temples. The design was so simple that workers were able to erect the entire structure in one day and complete the roofing in less than a week.

Pei's house-within-a-house perched on the hilltop made the most of the seasons. The interior core, snug against winter winds, was heated by radiant teak flooring and a fireplace. When warm weather arrived, slider after slider opened, removing walls and opening the interior to a screened deck that encircled the house. On rollers, the children's beds could easily be moved outside to make the most of the summer breezes and starlit nights. Pei described his getaway: "This was not a showpiece. We were raising young children."

Pei and his team worked on complicated large-scale projects that architects with far more experience would never have the opportunity to tackle. Pei had a hand in improving the lives of people in Boston, New York, Chicago, Cleveland, Denver, Washington D.C., Philadelphia, and Montreal. But after a decade of designing low-cost housing, Pei felt the need to grow as an architect, and he knew that he'd have to strike out on his own to do it. "I was doing a lot of low cost housing, a lot of urban redevelopment—exciting work, important work, but not the kind of work I really wanted to. I wanted to build concert halls, I wanted to do museums, I wanted to build public buildings, but as a house architect of a developer you just simply don't get that kind of opportunity. I knew that if I stayed within the envelope of the company, I would never get the kinds of jobs I wanted," Pei said.

It was at this restless time for Pei, in the late 1950s, that Zeckendorf found himself in financial trouble. The real estate market tanked, and Zeckendorf's creditors called in their loans. He couldn't cover his debts and was forced to declare bankruptcy. Pei sadly remembers, "In a way, Zeckendorf's financial problems were the beginning of my opportunity as an architect." With Zeckendorf's go-ahead, Pei opened his own architectural firm—first called I. M. Pei & Associates, and then later I. M. Pei & Partners.

This adventurous turning point in Pei's career wasn't the only cause for celebration in 1960. The three Pei boys now had a baby sister, Liane. The family was complete.

ASTRONOMER WALTER ORR ROBERTS AND I. M. PEI ENJOY EACH OTHER'S COMPANY OUTSIDE THE NATIONAL CENTER FOR ATMOSPHERIC RESEARCH, NCAR, IN BOULDER, COLORADO.

National Center for Atmospheric Research
Boulder, Colorado 1961-1967

Pei's first challenge was to find work for his new company. If the design world were a school playground, Pei would be the kid standing by himself by the fence. The "in crowd" of architects thought they were better than Pei, because Pei had been designing low-cost housing for years. In addition, rumors about Zeckendorf's financial problems hurt Pei. After all, Pei had been Zeckendorf's chief architect when the developer's business failed.

Fortunately, one rebel took a chance on Pei, an astronomer named Walter Orr Roberts. Roberts had a dream of building a think tank for scientists in the foothills of the Colorado Rockies. He imagined the National Center for Atmospheric Research, NCAR, sitting atop a mesa just outside the city of Boulder, Colorado. And he wanted Pei to build it.

Pei and Roberts walked through the site's meadow grass side by side, Roberts dressed in a wrinkled short-sleeved shirt, rumpled khakis, and scruffy sandals, Pei dressed in a pressed shirt, impeccably tailored jacket,

PEI'S INSPIRATION FOR NCAR CAME FROM AN ANCIENT SOURCE—THE THOUSAND-YEAR-OLD HONEYCOMBED PUEBLO CLIFF DWELLINGS.

and shiny leather shoes. The unlikely pair bonded over a shared passion for nature. Seated on an outcropping, sharing a bottle of wine, Roberts explained to Pei what he wanted from the building. He wanted a building that provided places for quiet contemplation, but also allowed for chance encounters among the scientists. A place where physicists could ponder cloud formations, chemists could meditate on the composition of the universe, and then they could share their thoughts with one another. "Walter Roberts was a very exceptional man," Pei said. "The reason I was attracted to him, and I think to a certain extent he was attracted to me, is because of my love of nature."

Pei came back to the site again and again—hiking through the craggy rocks and fragrant sage grass. He even spent one cold and soggy night in a sleeping bag, hoping the site would speak to him. Alone on the mesa, he thought about the mountaintop Buddhist retreats he'd experienced with his mother. "There in the Colorado Mountains," Pei said, "I tried to listen to the silence again—just as my mother had taught me."

Pei and his wife took a road trip through the Southwest, searching for inspiration. Pei found it in Mesa Verde National Park. There, hundreds of years ago, Pueblo Indians had built their honeycombed dwellings in the sandstone caves. "Here it is," Pei said. "A work of architecture that is at peace with nature."

Back at the mesa, Pei struggled to achieve the same blending of color and shape that the Pueblo Indians had managed. "The site is, indeed, the most beautiful we've ever had to deal with. You would think that, blessed with this kind of beauty, architecture would come easy. But it was not easy. We tried many buildings here, many, many designs, but they all fell apart. We didn't know why they fell apart until much later, when we discovered something we should have known all along, and that is that when you're confronted with nature—such power and beauty—you don't try to compete with it. You try to join with it, and this is exactly what we tried to do."

PEI INSPECTS THE COLOR OF TEST SLABS MADE OF CONCRETE AND STONE FOR THE NCAR BUILDING. HIS SELECTIONS BLEND INTO THE LANDSCAPE, THE SAME WAY AS THE PUEBLO DWELLINGS.

Pei crushed stone from a nearby quarry and mixed it with the concrete so that NCAR would have the same pink tones as the mountains around it. A bridge reaches out from NCAR, joining the building to a meadow planted with a special seed mixture chosen to match the wild grasses of the mesa. Staircases spiral to tower tops that scientists call their crows' nests. There, they escape to think about the air around them, to contemplate the ocean's floor or the sun's core. And on their way back to their desks, there's no telling who they might run into, for surprise encounters are possible at every turn.

Pei met the scientists' needs and did it in harmony with nature. For Pei this was the beginning of his journey toward finding his signature as an architect. He'd rediscovered his passion. He recalls, "I acquired an appetite for designing more—much more."

PEI'S FINISHED NCAR BUILDING NESTLES IN THE FOOTHILLS OF THE DRAMATIC COLORADO ROCKY MOUNTAINS, ECHOING THE RUGGED ROCK OUTCROPPINGS THAT RISE ABOVE IT.

National Center for Atmospheric Research

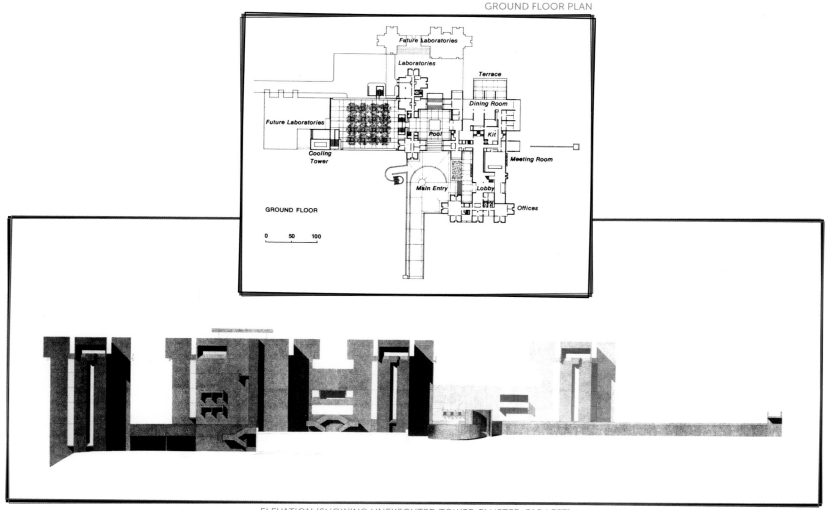

GROUND FLOOR PLAN

Future Laboratories

Laboratories

Terrace

Dining Room

Future Laboratories

Pool

Kit

Meeting Room

Cooling Tower

Main Entry

Lobby

Offices

GROUND FLOOR

0   50   100

ELEVATION (SHOWING UNEXECUTED TOWER CLUSTER, FAR LEFT)

28

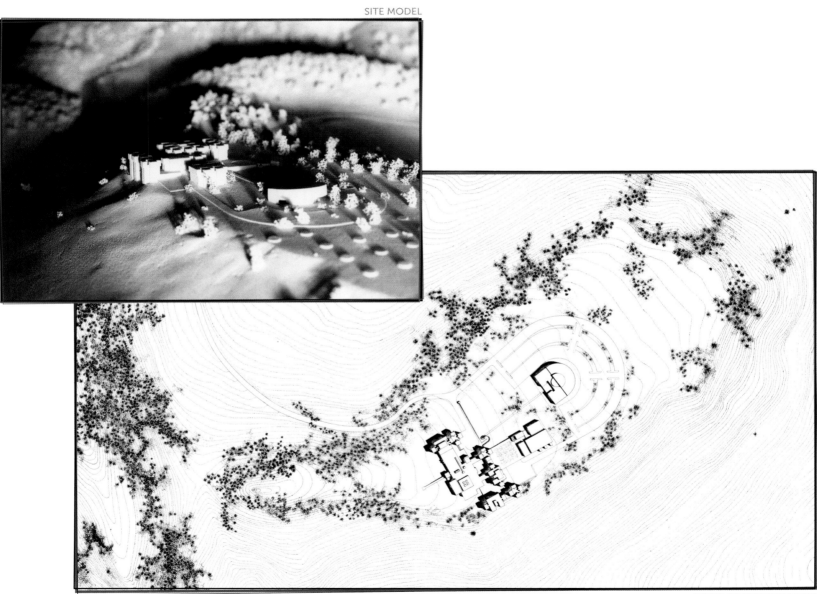

John F. Kennedy Presidential Library
Dorchester, Massachusetts 1964-1979

The most sought-after commission in 1964 was the John F. Kennedy Presidential Library. The nation, emerging from the shock of the assassination of a United States president and recovering from the grief of losing their young, vital hero, needed more than just a library to commemorate JFK. They needed a memorial—an architectural achievement that rivaled the great pyramids.

The world's finest architects were asked to vote for the architect they thought would best honor JFK's memory. For confidentiality, the ballots were counted and then burned. I. M. Pei was on the very short final list.

The president's widow, Jacqueline Kennedy, visited the nominated architects in each of their own offices. Pei prepared for her visit to his modest office space as if the queen of Egypt were coming. He repainted the walls. Tossed or hid all clutter. And dusted off and displayed some of his finest project models. All the architects in the firm were on their best behavior—no goofing off by rolling balls of tape from office to office. Many stood on tiptoe to get a glimpse of Mrs. Kennedy over the partitions.

When Jacqueline Kennedy asked Pei what kind of building he planned, Pei answered that it was too early to tell. This, above everything else, impressed Jacqueline Kennedy. The other architects had already made up their minds what the library should look like. Pei wanted his design to complement the location and to honor the man. Pei said, "I had to think about the president, what would he like it to be. I think that's number one."

Mrs. Kennedy was charmed by Pei the man as much as she was impressed by Pei the architect. "He was so full of promise, like Jack," she said. "They were born in the same year. I decided it would be fun to take a great leap with him." Two men, born in the Year of the Snake—whose careers soared as was prophesied.

Unfortunately, the project turned out to be anything but fun. The site chosen on the Charles River, across from JFK's alma mater, Harvard, belonged to the Massachusetts Bay Transportation

JACQUELINE KENNEDY SMILES AT SPEAKER I. M. PEI DURING THE DECEMBER 13, 1964 PRESS CONFERENCE ANNOUNCING A UNANIMOUS VOTE FOR PEI AS THE ARCHITECT FOR THE KENNEDY PRESIDENTIAL LIBRARY. KENNEDY AND PEI DEVELOPED A LIFELONG FRIENDSHIP DURING THE PROJECT.

CONSTRUCTION ON THE JOHN F. KENNEDY LIBRARY SUFFERED FROM MORE THAN A DECADE OF DELAYS. WITH THE ORIGINAL SITE IN CAMBRIDGE ADJACENT TO KENNEDY'S ALMA MATER, HARVARD, SCRAPPED, CONSTRUCTION BEGINS AT COLUMBIA POINT IN DORCHESTER, SOUTH OF BOSTON.

Authority. Subway tracks crisscrossed the storage yard which was littered with broken trolley cars. The site was twelve acres of eyesore, scarred with crumbling asphalt and tumbling repair sheds. Harvard was happy to have the blight disappear. Of course, no one else wanted to take the MBTA's dump. By the time the MBTA finally found a new place for storage, and cleared the lot, a different set of problems had cropped up.

Cambridge residents wanted the library, but not the museum. They saw JFK memorabilia—his sailboat, rocking chair, war mementos—as a crass amusement park attraction. Mrs. Kennedy's representative and trusted family friend, William Walton, grew discouraged when town meeting after town meeting ended in stalemate. The problems could have been resolved, but the people whom Walton called "the upper-class hippies" and "the Brattle Street elite" had no intention of trying to find solutions. They were only interested in showing off their political muscle.

Those opposed to building the presidential library at the Harvard site could have stonewalled construction for decades, and so the Kennedys looked elsewhere. They settled on Columbia Point, a site overlooking Boston Harbor. The site was far from perfect. It was a garbage dump, complete with a sewer pipe spewing millions of gallons of waste into the harbor. Pei said, "When we excavated, we found old sinks and old refrigerators and things of that kind. There was actually methane gas coming out of the soil. You can light a match on it and then it'd burn. It was that bad. I'm not exaggerating, it's true. So when I looked at it, I said, my gosh, from Harvard Yard to this site? It was quite a comedown. But we didn't give up."

Now more than a decade into the project, with funds dwindling, Pei designed the memorial at the new site. The building design was composed of three parts. Visitors would begin by entering one of two theaters to view a short film on the president's

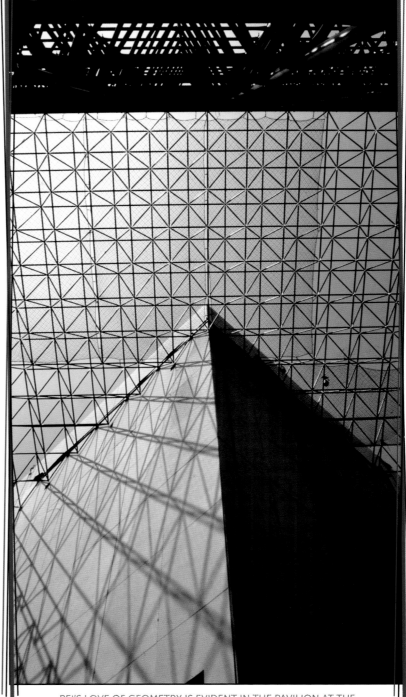

PEI'S LOVE OF GEOMETRY IS EVIDENT IN THE PAVILION AT THE JOHN F. KENNEDY LIBRARY.

THE FINISHED JOHN F. KENNEDY LIBRARY OVERLOOKS BOSTON HARBOR.

life. From there they would descend into the below-ground museum. From the darkened exhibition space, visitors finally surfaced into a 110-foot-high glass pavilion bathed in natural light—its sole adornment an American flag. At Jackie Kennedy's request, there was no bust of the president. Pei explained, "People coming from the exhibition don't want to see or hear any more, they just want silence. Their thoughts become the memorial."

With the design approved by his client, site preparation began. Pei sunk pilings 150 feet through the landfill to bedrock. He engineered drainage and venting to manage the sewage. And when he was done, he planted beach grass and wild roses—a Cape Cod landscape.

Fifteen years after the project had begun, the JFK Presidential Library opened. For Pei, the ceremonies must have been bittersweet. The commission which had catapulted his career through repeated endless delays and subsequent financial crises had taken its toll on Pei. "I lost my spirit," he said. "The whole project was for me tragic. It could have been so great."

The words inscribed on the wall of the atrium, taken from Kennedy's inaugural address, embrace not only Kennedy's spirit, but also the spirit of the building process. "All this will not be finished in the first one hundred days. Nor will it be finished in the first one thousand days, nor in the life of this Administration, nor even perhaps in our lifetime on this planet. But let us begin."

National Gallery of Art, East Building
Washington, D.C. 1968-1978

In a country where big is best, the National Gallery of Art deserved its share of superlatives—the biggest donation made to any government by a single person, the biggest marble building in the world. In a city where power is the currency, it took a man like Andrew Mellon to build on the Washington Mall, the most prized piece of real estate in the district, shared by such esteemed properties as the Lincoln and Jefferson memorials, the Washington Monument, and the Smithsonian's museums. Andrew Mellon, wealthy banker and industrialist, donated the funds to build the National Gallery and threw in 132 priceless works of art to kick off its collection.

When the National Gallery opened in 1941, Mellon's donations filled only five of the gallery's 135 rooms, but within three decades the collection grew to 30,000 pieces, all privately donated. The National Gallery had run out of space.

Andrew Mellon had the foresight to convince Congress to preserve nine grassy acres on the east side of the National Gallery for future expansion. Worried that Congress might renege on the promise, the gallery's director, John Walker, approached Andrew's son, Paul Mellon, president of the National Gallery since his father's death. Walker urged Mellon to proceed with the eastern addition to the gallery as soon as possible.

"How much?" Paul Mellon asked. Walker guessed twenty million. Paul Mellon pledged ten million. Paul's sister, Ailsa Mellon Bruce, pledged the second ten. And so the search for an architect began.

For decades the National Gallery had been rejecting Picassos and Matisses as "too modern." J. Carter Brown, the National Gallery's deputy director, hoped to change all that. He wanted a modern building. And for that he needed a modern architect. An architect who could also navigate volatile Washington politics. Who better than the diplomatic I. M. Pei?

Pei and Paul Mellon hit it off right from the start. They both had grown up with aloof banker

PEI MEETS WITH THE PRESIDENT OF THE NATIONAL GALLERY, PAUL MELLON (LEFT), AND THE DEPUTY DIRECTOR J. CARTER BROWN (CENTER) IN THE ATRIUM OF THE EAST BUILDING. OVERHEAD HANGS ALEXANDER CALDER'S UNTITLED MOBILE. THIS 920-POUND, 76-FOOT-LONG MOBILE, CALDER'S LAST MAJOR WORK, WAS INSTALLED ON NOVEMBER 18, 1977, ONE YEAR AFTER CALDER'S DEATH.

fathers. They both valued their privacy. They both loved art. Mellon understood when Pei drifted off into his own thoughts, drawing in the air on imaginary paper, oblivious to everything except the design developing in his head.

Pei knew from the start that this project would be difficult. He said, "This is probably the most sensitive site in the United States." It was unnerving, he said, "especially because the Mall is full of tradition and sacred to so many Americans."

Pei's first design concern was to make the East Building compelling for young people. "Otherwise," Pei said, "they will spend five minutes there and then go to the Air and Space Museum to look at the moon rocket. This is our problem. You have to think in terms of the public."

Fortunately, Pei had gained enormous experience thinking of the way the public uses space while working with Zeckendorf. Still, Pei spent many sleepless nights worrying about the odd-shaped lot and the connection necessary between the old gallery and new. "When I have to find the right design for a building it absorbs me completely. I can't think of anything else," Pei said. "This may be a matter of hours or it may take as long as a month of sleeping badly, being irritable, sketching ideas and rejecting them."

For the East Building, Pei's "aha moment" came while doodling during a flight back to New York from Washington. With a few slashes of red pen on the back of an envelope, the East Building was conceived. Pei sliced a trapezoid into two triangles, the lines of the old gallery matching up perfectly with the lines of the new.

Once the problem of the overall shape of the building was solved, Pei turned to the interior. Pei visited museums around the world and spoke with curators. He learned that museum visitors get tired after about 45 minutes. Pei estimated that 45 minutes translated into about 10,000 square feet of viewing. So Pei created

10,000-square-foot galleries in each corner of his triangular design. A light-filled atrium in the center gave visitors a chance to rest and digest what they had seen before moving on to the next gallery. Pei designed the ceilings on the top floors so that they could be raised and lowered depending on the scale of the exhibition. The detailed planning took three years.

In the spring of 1971, with I. M. and Eileen Pei watching from folding chairs, Paul Mellon turned the first shovel full of dirt in the groundbreaking ceremony. The challenges of constructing triangular buildings began. Pei would bring models of his design ideas to weekly meetings with the structural engineer and the builder.

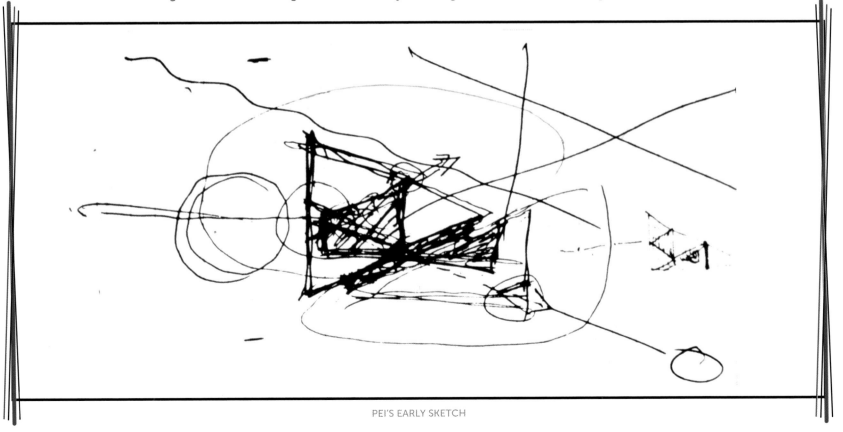

PEI'S EARLY SKETCH

SITE MODEL

"Can you build it?" Pei would ask.

"If you can design it," the builder would say to the structural engineer, "I can build it."

Carpenters, electricians, and plumbers accustomed to working with rectangles now faced a design without right angles. Undaunted, the builder called in surveyors to lay out struts, wire, and pipe. The architect who had chosen the marble for the National Gallery came out of retirement to choose the marble for the East Building. The slabs, quarried from the hills of Tennessee, were mapped out for installation. The darkest of the rose colored-marble were used to clad the concrete near the base of the building to give it a sense of solid footing.

There was no room in the budget for marble floors. So Pei decided to use concrete. But nothing short of a flawless finish would do for Pei. To make the concrete molds, cabinetmakers sanded thousands of feet of Douglas fir to a hand-rubbed finish and then discarded them after a single pour. Stonemasons crushed the Tennessee marble and mixed it with the concrete to match the color. Workers pounded the sides of the molds with wooden mallets to release bubbles in the concrete mud. When the mixture hardened, Pei inspected the unblemished, gleaming floor tiles and was satisfied with the result.

As construction dragged on, people visiting the Mall began to voice concern about the stark modern design. Washington residents worried that the triangular slab looked more like something out of a sci-fi movie than a stately building taking its place among national monuments. A Washington Post critic wrote, "What had seemed so dazzlingly clever on the cardboard model grew to seemingly monstrous proportions." Pei attempted to calm the growing discontent. "It's like a teenage girl with braces on her teeth. Wait until the scaffolding comes off."

And when the scaffolding did come off—it was love at first sight. Art critics raved. The public came in droves. Schoolchildren wrote thank you notes to Pei. On opening night at a star-studded black-tie dinner, Paul Mellon—surrounded by the artwork of modern masters—said, "Not the least of these great masters is I. M. Pei inside whose monumental contemporary sculpture you are all sitting at the moment." For Pei it was a moment to savor. As his grandfather had taught him so many years before: Wherever you go, go with your whole heart—and he had.

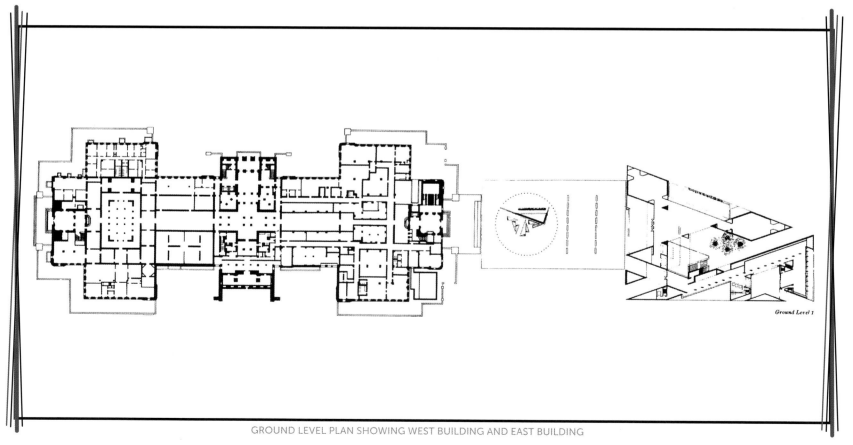

Ground Level 1

GROUND LEVEL PLAN SHOWING WEST BUILDING AND EAST BUILDING

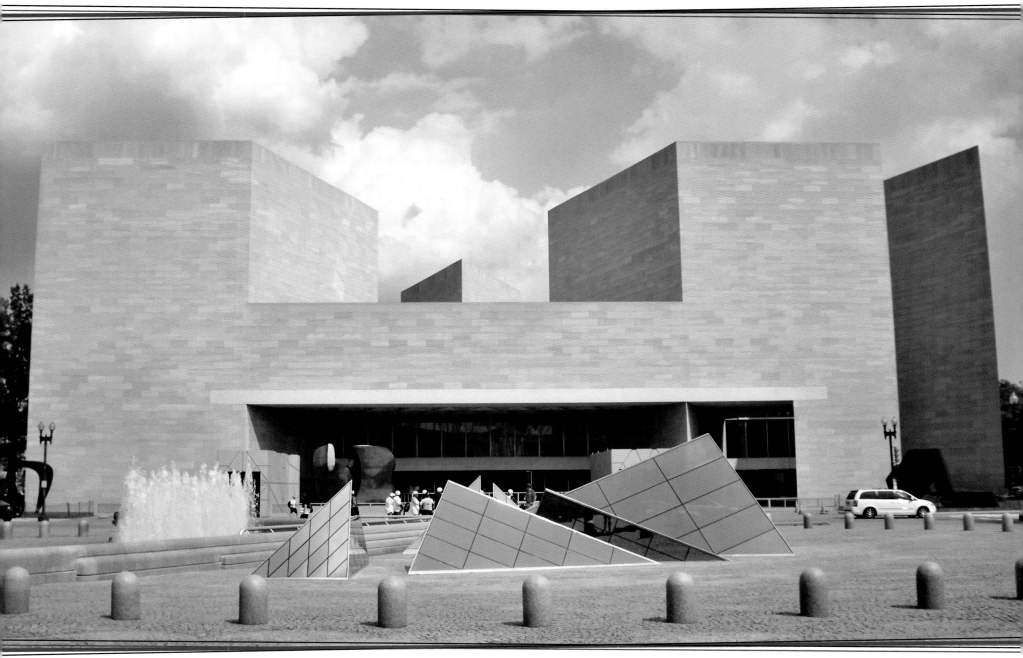

THE FRONT OF THE EAST BUILDING AS SEEN FROM THE MALL. A MASSIVE BRONZE SCULPTURE, *KNIFE EDGE MIRROR TWO PIECE*, BY HENRY MOORE, GRACES THE ENTRANCE.

Fragrant Hill Hotel
Beijing, China 1979-1982

Until the early 1970s, no one entered or left the People's Republic of China without permission from the government. And the government wasn't giving permission. Westerners were calling the barrier that separated communist East Asia from noncommunist states the bamboo curtain, a take-off on a similar barrier, the iron curtain, that had separated communist and noncommunist Europe after World War II.

Over the years, Pei had never given up hope of one day returning to China. He longed to hear the voices of his relatives and walk the winding pathways through the gardens in Suzhou where he had played as a child. The first cracks in the bamboo curtain came from an unexpected source—Ping-Pong. Despite the leveling caused by the Cultural Revolution, a Ping-Pong champion, Zhuang Zedong, rose in international stature. During training for the World Table Tennis Championship, Zhuang Zedong and an American team member became friends. This friendship led to the U.S. Ping-Pong team being invited to Beijing in 1971. And this Ping-Pong Diplomacy, as it became known, led to an invitation to the U.S. president, Richard Nixon, ten months later. The bamboo curtain had parted a smidgen and Pei was breathless with anticipation.

Pei's invitation to China came just six months after Nixon's. Although it would be nearly a year before Pei would make his first trip with a group of architects, the door had opened. Pei and his family could go home.

Pei discovered that the China he had held in his heart for nearly 40 years no longer existed. The ruthless effects of war had destroyed centuries-old buildings. And what bombs had failed to level, the communists had cemented over in artless utilitarian style. Even Pei's grandfather's gardens in Suzhou were not immune. They belonged to the people now. What must Pei have thought when he saw the garden rooms that had been designed for quiet meditation now trampled by hordes of littering tourists? There was no turning back for China. But did future builders have to clutter the landscape with soulless structures? Pei was determined to find a way to prevent that mistake. To make the old have new meaning. To bring the grace of ancient Chinese architecture into the twentieth century. To find the bridge to join his appreciation for China's history to his vision of modernism.

In 1978 Pei returned to China to meet with government officials as an adviser on city planning and development. Unlike 60-minute business meetings in the West where the pace is fast and the directive is to get to the point and stay on task, Chinese meetings are circuitous. There is tea, of course—lots of tea. And compliments followed by polite conversation. One only comes to the purpose of the meeting by the most indirect route. To take shortcuts in this process is rude, crass, uncivilized. Calling on all his Chinese-bred patience, instilled by his mother and reinforced by his grandfather, Pei sipped tea while searching for ways to discourage his Chinese hosts from taking a path that would lead to the ruin of some of Beijing's oldest and most historic buildings. Like his grandfather before him who had protected Suzhou, Pei now found himself in the role of protector of Beijing's Forbidden City, an imperial palace complex more than half a millennium old.

The Forbidden City, comprised of nearly 1,000 buildings spread over 250 acres, is the best-preserved example of ancient Chinese architecture anywhere. In the early years of the fifteenth century a million workers labored 15 years on the construction of the Forbidden City. Golden tiles paved the floors where thousands of concubines and courtiers served first the emperors of the Ming Dynasty and finally the emperors of the Qing Dynasty. The thought of this—the largest collection in the world of preserved ancient wood buildings—being dwarfed by high-rises of glass and steel was unacceptable to Pei. He repeatedly refused to undertake any project near the Imperial City's great walls and gates. "I just couldn't do it. My conscience wouldn't let me," Pei said. "If you destroy that sense of being alone, of being an object by itself, then you destroy the artifact."

Chinese officials were determined to convince Pei to lead them into the modern world with modern style. Later that year they approached Pei once again. They invited Pei's entire family to spend the Christmas holiday in China. Pei and Eileen, their three sons T'ing, Didi, and Sandi; their daughter, Liane; and their two grandchildren, Alyssa and five-month-old Stephen, flew to Beijing. In Beijing the Peis were wooed by Chinese officials. One banquet followed another. As they traveled from one event to the next, the Chinese people gawked at them. It was not the famous architect who drew their stares, however. It was the Pei children. T'ing explains their fascination: "At the time, everybody in China wore blue cotton jackets. We were dressed in colorful ski parkas. They couldn't figure out if we were Chinese or what." Pei's daughter, Liane, adds that even their own relatives found them curious. "They were horrified that we couldn't speak Chinese. We could only smile stupidly at them. We couldn't communicate."

When Pei—again—refused to build near the Forbidden City, officials relented and suggested alternative sites. A few days before Christmas, Pei and his son and partner Didi set off to explore one of the sites located outside the city. A fresh blanket of snow draped the walls of the park surrounding what was once the emperor's private hunting grounds. Bitter winter winds buffeted Pei and Didi as they climbed Fragrant Hill to survey the site. But Pei hardly noticed winter's bite. "I didn't even hesitate. I said, 'Let's build here.'"

This commission was not a grand structure, the kind Pei was accustomed to building. Fragrant Hill was to be a low-rise hotel—elegant but small. A place for foreigners to stay now that China had pulled back the bamboo curtain and for Chinese visitors to stay as well—a place true to Chinese hospitality and sensibilities. Nor was the client a strong individual with distinct tastes like those Pei had worked with in the past, such as Paul Mellon or Jackie Kennedy. Pei felt his work at Fragrant Hill must represent the Chinese people—they were to be his client. Even Pei's vision was nothing like anything he had done before. The pure geometry of modernism he'd applied elsewhere was not enough for Fragrant Hill. Reflecting on what had led him to its design, Pei said, "Chinese architects . . . couldn't go back to the old way. The days of the temples and the palaces are not only economically out of reach but ideologically unacceptable to them. They've tried the Russians' way, and they hate those buildings. They are trying now to take the Western way. I am afraid that will be equally unacceptable. I would like in a small way to pay a debt to the culture from which I came, to try and help them search for a new way."

Pei's search for a new way began like so many of his other projects—by exploring the area and absorbing the details around him. He spoke to shopkeepers and farmers. He wandered through moon gates into private and public gardens. He sipped tea in courtyards exchanging views with ordinary families. "Architecture," Pei said, "has to come out of people's homes. I would not look for Italian roots in Michelangelo's work in the Vatican. I would go to Florence to look at the houses where people live."

FRAGRANT HILL PLAN SHOWS A PERSPECTIVE OF THE HOTEL WITH A TRADITIONAL CHINESE LANDSCAPE PAINTING.

Pei may not have heard the bamboo sprouting as he once did on a mountainside with his mother, but he did hear the crunch of pebbles on pathways, the rustle of branches in the wind, and the trickle of water coursing over stone sculptures. These features all found their way into Pei's Fragrant Hill design.

Pei's greatest influence came from his grandfather's gardens in Suzhou that he had loved as a child. "A Chinese garden is like a maze," Pei explains. "You never see straight or clear to the end, never apprehend the whole. You enter, something attracts your attention, so you pause. It might be just a single tree or a rock or crevice of light. Then you move further on a path or perhaps across a bridge, zigging and zagging, so you always see something different, the delight of the unexpected."

Like the Chinese garden, Pei planned for the hotel at Fragrant Hill to take unexpected twists and turns, a style Chinese folklore claims to confuse wandering ghosts. Guest wings zig and zag outward from a central atrium. The hotel shifts direction to preserve two 800-year-old ginko trees. Gardens—eleven of them—appear and delight, framed by unusual-shaped windows. Pei said, "In the West, a window is a window. It lets in light and fresh air. But to the Chinese, it's a picture frame. And the garden is always there."

Satisfied that he had captured the essence of the old—a reverence for nature and cultural history—and had expressed it through the simplicity of the new, Pei presented a detailed model of Fragrant Hill to Chinese officials. Normally, at this juncture, Pei would assign designers to handle the project. Although Pei would check in from time to time, the day-to-day work would be handled by his deputies. Not so with Fragrant Hill. With Fragrant Hill, Pei hoped to convey to Chinese architects a language of their own rather than an imitation of foreign architecture. "China is a country with a long history and a deep culture," Pei said. "Its architecture should grow naturally from its own past."

From the very beginning Fragrant Hill was plagued with problems. Pei's representative in China, Kellogg Wong, was hustling to the airport to fly home to attend his daughter's high school graduation when he received an urgent call from New York. Pei told Wong that when Chinese surveyors had traced the hotel's outline on the ground with ashes, it revealed that 112 mature trees would have to come down—cypresses, chestnuts, cedars, pines, willows, and ginkos all would have to be felled. Pei had specifically designed the hotel to preserve as many of these gnarly works of art as possible. Something must be wrong.

Wong rushed to the site. He discovered the surveyors had made an error. They had oriented the hotel from an incorrect starting point. Yet even when the corrections were made, Wong was alarmed to see that there were still far too many doomed trees. Wong worked all night, bent over the site plans, desperate to find ways to save the most valuable of the trees. He added even more zigs and zags to Pei's original design. No ghost was going to find his way down these corridors. Blurry eyed from a sleepless night, Wong presented the new plans to the Chinese surveyors and engineers. They were delighted. The new design preserved the maximum amount of the treasured trees. From that moment on, they affectionately called Pei's representative Save-the-Tree Mr. Wong.

With associates from Pei's firm on-site, and Pei's son Didi overseeing the project design, groundbreaking began—and with it more problems. The spirit of the Cultural Revolution where equality reigns may be noble in theory, but in practice it fosters chaos. No individual could assume the role of "boss." Those who normally would have authority in a project in the United States had none in China. Workers had the same clout as architects and engineers. Every decision was subject for debate. A foreman could hold up an entire day's work through sheer stubbornness if he wished. Pei remembers that construction at Fragrant Hill was "one of the most difficult

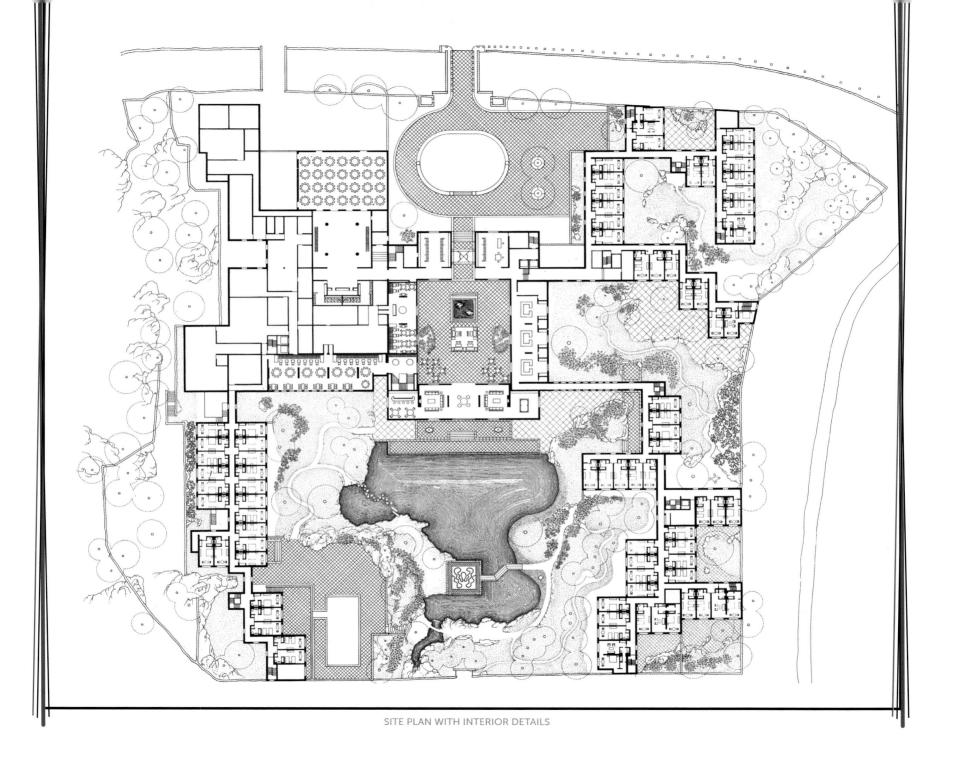

SITE PLAN WITH INTERIOR DETAILS

experiences I've ever had, a mixture of elation and frustration, trying to work in a system I did not understand. We could not give orders, only advice, and the Chinese do not make decisions lightly."

What's more, China had not yet caught up with the technology of the Western world. Boulders were dislodged by donkeys, rolled onto bamboo slings, and carried away by hand or in donkey carts. Foundations were dug with shovels. Concrete was mixed and poured by hand. The Chinese may not have had the modern tools, but they had the manpower—and lots of it. Two thousand workers shoveled with such vigor that they dug the foundation two stories too deep. Efforts that would have taken American construction workers a week with all their fancy equipment were accomplished by Chinese workers in a single day through sheer numbers.

Although there was no shortage of unskilled laborers to perform brute tasks, artisans who practiced traditional Chinese arts and crafts were nearly nonexistent. Not only had communism in China removed hierarchy in the workplace, it had also removed any support for the practice of ancient craftsmanship. Skills no longer practiced were all but lost. Pei could have imported artisans and materials, but that would not have stayed true to the spirit of Fragrant Hill. Pei wanted traditional Chinese materials crafted in the traditional Chinese manner. Finding artisans who still used ancient methods was a challenge. One of Pei's associates, graphic designer Tracy Turner, scoured the countryside and manufacturing plants searching for those who might remember the old ways. When Pei expressed his desire to trim windows in a tile that hadn't been produced in two centuries, fired in kilns that had been long closed, miraculously his designers were able to recruit a craftsman in his seventies who had learned the tricks of creating the tile's distinctive sheen as a child.

Sometimes it wasn't the craft that challenged Pei's designers. It was the materials. In order to achieve a sense of serenity and a connection to nature, no detail was too small for consideration. Even the pebbles that lined the pathways snaking through the gardens were chosen with care. Pei was determined to acquire pebbles that came from a riverbed running along the Vietnam border in a place so remote it could only be accessed by mule. The villagers there were so delighted to see their first foreigner, they slaughtered a pig in Pei's associate's honor. But the associate misunderstood their intentions. "There was blood everywhere. I thought, They're going to kill me. . . ."

Once the villagers discovered the associate's reason for trekking to their far corner of the world, all thoughts of roast pig fled. "They were astounded that this foreigner was going to give them thousands of dollars for pebbles. All the grandmothers and kids descended on the stream."

That wasn't the only adventure involving rocks. One of Pei's primary objectives was to express the importance of the relationship between architecture and nature. Just as his grandfather's garden in Suzhou had rocks as sculpture, Pei wanted to use rocks as sculpture at Fragrant Hill. But Fragrant Hill's scale was much larger than the private garden of a home owner. Finding rocks large enough posed a problem. On a flight to Beijing, Pei happened to be flipping through a travel brochure when he stumbled on the solution. The article was about a 2,000,000-year-old stone forest in a part of China so secluded it was named Beyond the Clouds. These weathered-by-nature pillars were exactly what Pei envisioned for his gardens at Fragrant Hill—they even matched the tiles being fired for the window trim. Pei was so excited about his discovery, he telephoned his associates at Fragrant Hill while waiting in line at customs right after landing.

The stones may have been the perfect touch for Fragrant Hill's gardens, but one doesn't just enter a national park and remove monoliths—not even I. M. Pei. It took a year of negotiations—and a lot of tea—to obtain permission. Once the particular rocks had been chosen, workers loaded 40 flatbed train cars with 230

STONE MONOLITHS SERVE AS SCULPTURAL ELEMENTS IN FRAGRANT HILL HOTEL'S GARDEN.

tons of monoliths. Although one-third of them were broken during the 2,000-mile journey to Fragrant Hill, those that survived the trip lent just the other-worldy aura Pei had been hoping for.

Not all the stones used at Fragrant Hill had to travel so far. One treasured stone was found right at the construction site. This marble slab called a liu shui yin was one of only five remaining in all of China, one of which is in the Forbidden City. A liu shui yin is a water sculpture. Water flows along a 165-foot-long switch-backed channel carved into the length of the stone. Legend has it that on moonlit nights poets floated wine glasses down the channel. They were allowed to drink the wine only if they had composed a poem before

their wine glass reached the end. The liu shui yin at Fragrant Hill sits in the middle of a pond teeming with goldfish, which in China represent gold and abundance, yet another traditional Chinese symbol Pei incorporated into his design.

During the summer of 1979, Pei's team made a final push to ready Fragrant Hill for its October opening. Interior finish work brought a fresh set of problems. Workers unfamiliar with modern conveniences plastered

GLASS CEILINGS IN FRAGRANT HILL HOTEL'S LOBBY BRING NATURAL LIGHT INTO THE SPACE.

walls before installing wiring and connected bathroom ventilation to air-conditioning ducts. Pei's associate scrambled to rectify the mistakes, saying, "It stunk to high heaven."

Originally, experienced hoteliers were to manage the hotel. But instead, Chinese officials awarded the job to a loyal Communist Party veteran—one with no hotel experience. No training was provided to local workers who were accustomed to dirt floors and no running water. When the Peis arrived a few days before the opening, they were horrified. The carpets were filthy, the toilets dirty. The beds had not been made nor the curtains hung. Garbage littered the stairwells and paint stained the marble floors. Frantic, the Peis and designers rolled up their sleeves and set to work. I. M. Pei got down on his hands and knees to scrape paint off the floor tiles while Eileen Pei made beds and vacuumed. "I was so tired at one point that I burst into tears," Eileen said.

On October 17, 1979, Fragrant Hill opened with a parade of VIPs from all over the world, elbow to elbow with Chinese officials. After touring the hotel, one vexed official told Pei, "It looks Chinese." With a resigned shrug, Pei took it as the compliment it was not meant to be.

A decade later, Fragrant Hill was falling apart from neglect. The gardens Pei had so lovingly designed looked bedraggled and unkempt. Pei shrugged once again. "They are not doing the wrong things on purpose," Pei said. "They are once removed from the farms and the trenches." Pei's associate Kellogg Wong is hopeful. "I. M.'s legacy to Chinese architecture is one China will one day awaken to." In the meantime, Pei comforted himself with the thought that he had succeeded in his guardianship of China's most honored real estate. The Chinese government adopted a new city-development ordinance. No tall building could be constructed where it would overshadow the Forbidden City. "This more than anything," Pei said, "is my greatest contribution to China."

FRAGRANT HILL HOTEL'S STRONG, GEOMETRIC DESIGN IS MODERN WHILE RESPECTING CHINA'S ARCHITECTURAL PAST.

Bank of China
Hong Kong 1982-1989

In 1982, two emissaries from the Bank of China traveled to New York City. Great Britain's 99-year lease on Hong Kong would end on July 1, 1997, and on the eve of June 30 Great Britain was to return Hong Kong to China. The Chinese government decided it would be wise to assure the residents of Hong Kong that the communist government was financially secure. What better way to demonstrate that strength than to build a bank designed to evoke confidence and stability? And who better to build it than the most famous architect of Chinese descent? But custom did not allow the officials to approach I. M. Pei directly. First they must speak to Pei's father, Tsuyee, and get his permission.

One would think Tsuyee Pei, who had lobbied for the construction of the original Hong Kong branch more than six decades earlier and had been its first manager, would be the perfect person to consult. But the Chinese government was communist now, and Tsuyee had joined Chiang Kai-shek to fight the communists—the communists who had seized his bank. I. M. Pei explains, "This is Chinese, very respectful even though they were politically at odds." Tsuyee told the officials that they should ask his son, that to build or not to build was up to him.

Office buildings never had much appeal for Pei. Occupants are here today, gone tomorrow. "When the lease runs out, someone else moves in," Pei said. And more than half of this building was slated for rental. Nor did he care much for skyscrapers. Nothing distinguished them. Height was their only remarkable feature. To make matters even less desirable, the site that the Bank of China had already purchased was a miserable postage stamp of land on an awkward slope, surrounded by elevated highways, and situated so that the entrance would have to face a grungy parking garage.

The deplorable site wasn't the only challenge. The proposed budget was modest at best. And it was a fraction of the dollars per square foot being spent constructing a competing bank on prime real estate nearby. Pei was all too aware that the other bank's design would surely be compared to his own when both projects were completed. Although no one came straight out and said it, the message was loud and clear—the Bank of China's branch had to outshine its rival. "After the budget was set, one did not go back to the People's Congress and ask for more. China was a poor country; anything more would have been extravagant. So I never asked," Pei said.

Pei did have two requests, however. The first was a land swap with an adjacent government property. One corner of their lot in exchange for one corner of the site. This trade would reshape the Bank of China's lot into a parallelogram. Now Pei could rotate the building so that it no longer faced the ugly parking garage and instead faced a lovely public garden. He could also incorporate triangular gardens into the site plan. His second condition for taking on the project was that he be allowed to put in a new road. This new road would join with city streets, making it easier to approach the bank. One of Pei's primary concerns when siting a building is its approach, not only for ease of access, but also for the experience an elegant approach can provide the visitor. These two conditions were critical to Pei. He said, "If a building is not properly sited, no matter how beautiful, or how well it functions, it will not have the right context. Siting is the first major step toward architecture."

Once these conditions were met, Pei began his process of discovering the design that best suited the site. Those around him were all too familiar with this process, especially Eileen and their children. By now they were used to this stage when Pei talked to himself, tossed and turned through sleepless nights, and walked around as if in another world. One weekend at their country getaway in Katonah, New York, Pei's son Sandi watched his father play with sticks, holding four in his fist. Pei slid the sticks up and down, varying the heights. He pushed and pulled until he found an arrangement that pleased him. Each stick extended one-quarter the total length beyond the next. Sandi said, "My father has a way of working in isolation before summoning any associates. It was like watching the whole thing unfold in front of me."

Back at the firm in New York City, Sandi arranged for the company's model makers to cut a single block of wood into four pieces by slicing it on the diagonals lengthwise. Pei, sliding these pieces in the same way he had slid the sticks, was able to demonstrate the four-stepped arrangement that he had imagined for the Bank of China. When he presented the idea to a structural engineer, Leslie Roberston, who had worked on many complicated designs including the World Trade towers, Roberston was astounded. Here was an entirely new way to build skyscrapers. Not only was it novel, it was brilliant structurally. Roberston said, "It represented a new way of building. It opened people's minds to the importance of structure in architecture."

Tall buildings have many structural challenges. One obvious challenge is weight. The more floors you pile on top of one another, the more weight rests on each floor below. This requires massive steel supports. Another challenge is wind. In Hong Kong, typhoons make the challenge even greater than in most cities. The bracing must be twice as strong as a building erected in the windy city of Chicago, and four times that used in Los Angeles to combat tremors from earthquakes. All this extra steel is costly. In Pei's innovative design using diagonals, all the weight—both lateral and vertical—was shifted to the four corners. This reduced the amount of steel needed for internal support by 40 percent—a considerable savings. Pei said, "If you only have so much money you spend it on the essentials. I knew that if we could find economy in structure, we would have an economical building. Structure, in fact, was the generating force behind the design, even before we had an engineer."

Pei found another way to save money and meet his limited budget. Normally steel members are welded at the joints. Welding is an expensive, time-consuming method when there are thousands of connections to be made. Instead, Pei joined his steel girders with concrete. "It's almost like a giant drop of glue," Pei explained. "It is in the union of technology and design that architecture has its fullest potential."

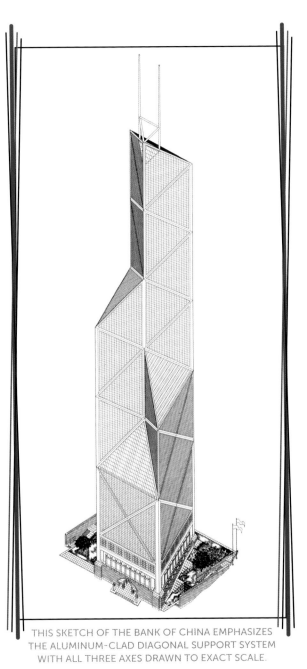

THIS SKETCH OF THE BANK OF CHINA EMPHASIZES THE ALUMINUM-CLAD DIAGONAL SUPPORT SYSTEM WITH ALL THREE AXES DRAWN TO EXACT SCALE.

While Pei was in New York working on the Bank of China's design, rumors spread through Hong Kong. The location that the Chinese government had chosen for the Bank of China had a ghastly history. During World War II, the site had been the headquarters for a Japanese military unit. There, Chinese prisoners had been tortured and executed. The people of Hong Kong feared that the ghosts of these prisoners haunted the site. The ghoulish rumors were only reinforced when Pei's initial design was unveiled. Rather than hide the diagonal braces, Pei chose to highlight them by cladding them in polished aluminum. The giant aluminum X's created by the cladding carried their own frightful meaning. To the Chinese, this was the mark of a condemned man, his fate made public by a sign worn around his neck bearing his name, with a bold X that crossed it out.

Feng shui masters found no shortage of chilling omens in Pei's design. Feng shui, which means "wind-water" in Chinese, is an ancient art for orienting buildings—everything from tombs to skyscrapers. Although the communists had tried to suppress feng shui during the Cultural Revolution of the 1960s by claiming it to be pure superstition, many Chinese hung on to the tradition. Feng shui masters were often consulted and paid substantial fees to ensure the prospective building was best positioned to cultivate a positive chi—or life force. Perhaps feeling a bit jilted because they were not consulted, the feng shui masters claimed Pei's building had serious issues. Parallel masts that topped the building were likened to a pair of chopsticks upright in an empty rice bowl, a symbol of poverty. The sharp corners resembled knife blades and threatened the bank's neighbors, their pointed edges sure to unleash demons from the underworld. And the waterfalls that Pei had planned meant that wealth and prosperity would flow away—definitely not good tidings for a bank.

When Pei discovered how seriously the people of Hong Kong took feng shui, he arranged for an associate to study the principles of the ancient system and how it applied to his design. "Feng shui masters are like lawyers here, they're everywhere. I knew I'd have trouble, but I didn't know what kind of trouble to expect," Pei said. In an "if you can't beat them, join them" move, Pei cast his own interpretations on his design. The building, he said, was like bamboo after the spring rains. Each step a joint, pushing upward, a symbol of strength, excellence—and for Hong Kong soon to be back in China's fold—renewal, and hope. By hiding the horizontal bracing behind the glass face of the building, those X's suddenly turned into diamonds—a most auspicious shape for a bank. And addressing the superstitions regarding the soil supposedly tainted by monstrous wartime acts, Pei turned to an ancient Chinese proverb about a lotus plant which grows from the mucky pond bottom to blossom into a pure and unscathed flower on the water's surface. The building, he hoped, would do the same.

Although sentiments toward Pei's building were shifting, there were those who still felt uneasy. Neighboring residents hung mirrors outside their doors and windows and from their balcony railings to deflect demonic forces that carried bad luck wherever they went. To keep dragons away, workers kept vigil burning incense in shrines scattered around the perimeter of the building.

SOME SUGGESTED THE MASTS ON TOP OF THE BANK OF CHINA BUILDING WERE SYMBOLS OF STICKS OF INCENSE HONORING THE DEAD, OTHERS INTERPRETED THE MASTS AS CHOPSTICKS STICKING OUT OF AN EMPTY RICE BOWL.

Pei continued to battle feng shui prophesies. His efforts were not limited to proverbs and analogies. Remembering his father's admonition that a bank must not only be secure, it must look that way, too, Pei designed a three-story granite base for the bank that could only be interpreted as rock-solid, rooted—secure. Within, a grand banking hall added an elegant note, more assurance to customers and clients of the bank's solvency. And those waterfalls? Pei changed their direction so they no longer represented money flowing out. Now they enhanced the chi by camouflaging traffic noise with the sound of gentle splashes.

China is a country with many traditions. There are even traditions involving construction. It is customary to have a ceremony when the last piece of framing is put into place. How fortunate that this stage of construction coincided with what many believed to be the luckiest day of the century. In Cantonese the word for prosperity is *faat,* and is very similar to the word for eight, *baat*. Therefore, there was no luckier day in the twentieth century to be born—or to hold a ceremony—than the eighth day of the eighth month of the year 1988. And so, on August 8, 1988, open-air, wire-meshed construction elevators loaded with scores of dignitaries and guests shuddered up the Bank of China's 70 stories. There, the last beam, engraved with the names of all the workmen on the project, lay on the cement floor ready to be bolted into place. Hundreds of colored balloons scattered skyward, drifting along with the smoke from burning incense while revelers drank sake and dined on roast pig. For one brief moment, all looked hopeful. At last, a new China was emerging from the dark years of its recent past like the lotus blossom rising from the murky pond bottom—or so everyone thought.

On the eve of June 3, 1989, everything changed. For months, Chinese students and intellectuals had been demonstrating in Beijing. It began when an outspoken proponent for reform, Hu Yaobang, died. One hundred thousand mourners gathered in Tiananmen Square on the eve of Hu's funeral. Students built shrines

THE BANK OF CHINA SOARS UNDER CONSTRUCTION, PROVIDING WORKERS WITH A DRAMATIC VIEW OF HONG KONG'S HARBOR.

in his honor. They wrote moving eulogies. But soon what began as collective mourning shifted to collective unrest. Now rather than eulogies the students drafted demands. They spoke out against authoritarianism and spoke up for democracy. They petitioned the government to revisit the reforms Hu had championed. Rallies soon sprouted up all over the country. Sit-ins were staged. Teachers boycotted classes. But the largest group,

TENSION ESCALATES BETWEEN SOLDIERS AND DEMONSTRATORS IN CHINA'S TIANANMEN SQUARE DURING THE STUDENT UPRISING IN 1989.

the most vocal protesters, met in Tiananmen Square just outside the Forbidden City. Working men and women marched with the protesters, singing patriotic songs in the spirit of solidarity. Thousands of students went on to stage a hunger strike until their demands were met.

The Chinese government was split. But by early June, those sympathetic to the students had been ousted. The remaining Communist Party leaders ordered the military to put a stop to the protests. The People's Liberation Army advanced on Tiananmen Square. What happened next is not certain. The estimates of the number of unarmed civilians shot and killed vary from the Chinese government's estimate of a few hundred to the Soviet government's estimate of 10,000. There are chilling photographs of tanks lined up in an empty Tiananmen Square in the aftermath of the massacre. They do not offer a picture of hope or renewal. Workers at Pei's Bank of China in Hong Kong draped an enormous black banner across the building. In Chinese letters it read, "Blood for Blood. Long Live Democracy."

Back in his offices in New York City, Pei was distraught. "It hurt me very deeply because doing this building was an expression of confidence in this country." He could no longer look at his gift to the new Hong Kong without feeling betrayed. Pei, normally an extremely private man, was moved to speak publicly against the senseless bloodshed. He, with his wife Eileen, wrote an op-ed piece for *The New York Times*. In it they expressed their devotion and connection to the United States as their adopted home and China as their birthplace. "As I worked with a new generation of Chinese, my hopes for the future of China were ever more optimistic. We believed that China was gradually emerging from its long nightmare of war and repression. We saw a new generation of young men and women, less scarred by the terrible history of the country, coming into their own. I worked with them closely, and sometimes they shared with me their hopes for themselves and their country.

We wanted to believe that a more open and modern China was possible. Today, those dreams are dashed by the horrible events of Tiananmen Square."

Pei wrote that the "killing of students and citizens tore the heart out of a generation that carries the hope for the future," and his words made it clear that his own heart was torn out as well. The title of the piece was "China Won't Ever Be the Same." It is doubtful that I. M. Pei would be either.

Louvre

Paris, France
Phase I: 1983-1989, Phase II: 1989-1993

In the early 1980s, the Louvre in Paris, France, deserved the title "National Disgrace" more than "National Treasure." Over the previous eight centuries it had been used as a palace, fortress, barracks, prison, and even as a hayloft. The quarter-mile-long Grande Galerie had served as everything from Napoleon's wedding aisle, when he married the archduchess of Austria, to Louis XIII's racetrack, when he rode a miniature carriage pulled by two mastiffs. But for the previous hundred years, like Sleeping Beauty's castle, neglect had led to its ruin.

As a museum, the Louvre was a disaster. With little gallery space and even less storage room, the Louvre was forced to lend out most of its collection. Artwork hung in poorly lit galleries, the frames felted with dust. If the curator wished to remove a painting, he was forced to lower it out the window. The yearly three million visitors had trouble navigating the poorly laid-out floor plan. And for all those guests, there were only two public rest rooms. The French minister of culture, Emile Biasini, said, "If it was to continue as a museum, it was absolutely necessary to do something. The Louvre was in a grave condition. It was the world's most miserable museum."

The newly elected French president, François Mitterrand, doubled France's budget for the arts. He hoped to stimulate a cultural awakening through extensive building—his *grands projets*—to modernize Paris. And the grandest project of them all was the remodeling of the Louvre.

Mitterrand appointed Biasini to direct the Louvre's renovation. Biasini began by searching for just the right architect for the job. "I wanted someone capable of respecting history, but innovative enough to attack anew," he said.

For nine months, Biasini traveled from museum to museum all over Europe and the United States. Everywhere he went, he asked the curators to recommend the architect who would do the best job of renovating the Louvre. "Pei was on every list," Biasini said. Biasini felt Pei's Chinese heritage gave him a profound appreciation of the importance of the past, and his American experience had taught him how best to utilize modern public space. Pei fit Biasini's requirements perfectly.

When Mitterrand and Biasini offered Pei the project, Pei was honored but could not accept at first. Pei asked if they'd give him four months to study the Louvre and its history before making his decision. "I'd already decided I wanted to do this," Pei said, but he wanted some time, "to see if I could in fact do it."

Pei flew to Paris three times. He wandered the galleries and corridors of the Louvre. He walked along the Seine. Hands clasped behind his back, he peered through his trademark round eyeglasses at Napoleon's grand courtyard, now reduced to a parking lot. He imagined the public coming—hundreds of people, thousands of people. How would they enter? How would they move from gallery to gallery? How could he elevate the visitors' experience from a confusing ordeal to an event worthy of the art treasures displayed inside? After days of deliberation, Pei said, "I concluded that it had to be done, and that I would be able to do it."

Pei eagerly returned to his New York office, where he sequestered himself on the eighth floor, installed locks, and proceeded to design the Louvre's renovation as if it were a tightly kept state secret. He studied the work of André Le Notré, France's legendary landscape architect who, under King Louis XIV, designed the gardens of Versailles. Le Notré's use of open space, geometry, light, and water appealed to Pei's similar sensibilities.

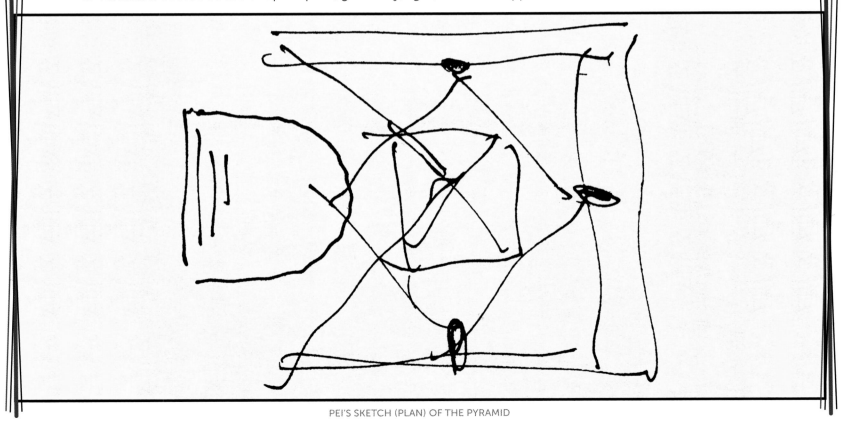

PEI'S SKETCH (PLAN) OF THE PYRAMID

Pei had decided while in Paris that the only acceptable entrance was through the Louvre's center of gravity, which lay in Napoleon's courtyard. From there, visitors would be equidistant from the Louvre's three wings, making movement throughout the galleries efficient. Not wanting to take away from the regal presence of the Louvre's architecture, Pei's enormous addition would be completely underground. To avoid a subway-entrance atmosphere, Pei planned to flood the entrance and passageways with light. The challenge was to do it in a way that complemented the existing buildings.

Applying his love for pure geometric shapes, Pei decided on pyramids—three small glass pyramids (one upside down)—to light the passageways to the wings and one large glass pyramid over the entrance. After experimenting with different angles for the pyramid sides, Pei discovered that the Egyptians "had been right four thousand years ago. A few degrees steeper and it's too aggressive, a few degrees less and it seems to melt away."

Pei's subterranean addition addressed all the problems that faced the museum—the lack of storage space, the need for restoration facilities, public spaces for shops and cafés and lecture rooms. Pei even incorporated tunnels equipped with electric carts for moving masterpieces—no more lowering them out the windows. The increased square footage would make the Louvre the world's largest museum.

His design not only managed the flow of people through the museum, but in the streets outside as well. Finding the entrance would no longer be a problem. The shabby parking area would be transformed into a pleasant courtyard with seven fountains and reflecting pools.

On January 23, 1984, Pei unveiled his plans to the ministry of culture. He was ambushed. Members read prepared statements denouncing a plan they had never seen before. The attacks were so nasty, Pei's translator

THE GRAND STAIRWAY BRINGS VISITORS TO THE LOUVRE'S UNDERGROUND LOBBY.

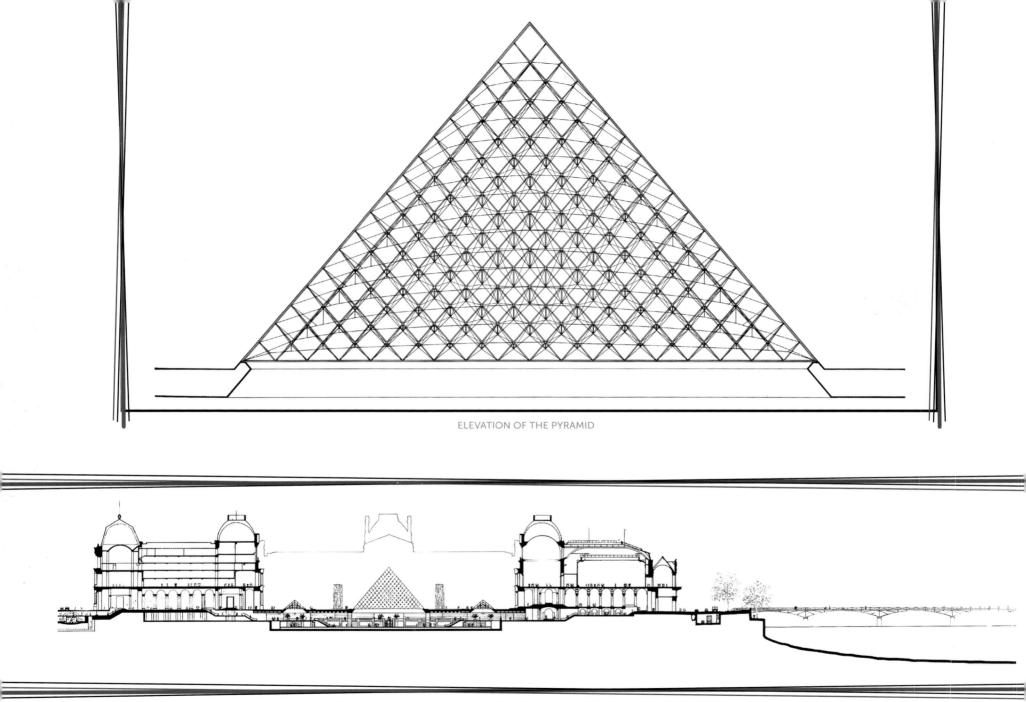

ELEVATION OF THE PYRAMID

NORTH-SOUTH SECTION SHOWING PYRAMID, UNDERGROUND SPACES, AND PAVILIONS

broke into tears and could not go on. From the beginning, the French were not happy that a foreigner would be undertaking the transformation of a building close to the geographic heart of Paris and the emotional heart of Parisians. Now they unleashed their wrath. Pei's daughter, Liane, remembers a French woman spitting on her father in the street. Pei's co-workers remember the pressure they felt back in the New York office. It was, they said, "mind-boggling, shells were landing all over." Through it all, Pei never appeared distraught. With the grace of a diplomat, he persevered.

President Mitterand weathered much of the same opposition. The French disliked the pyramid so much they took to wearing protest buttons. The press likened Mitterand to Egypt's pharaoh Ramses with headlines such as "Mitterramses I and His Pyramid." Mitterand's approval rating dropped right along with Pei's. And yet Mitterand's support for Pei did not waver. Despite curators dubbing Mitterand's grand projects "grand monsters," he remained determined and single-mindedly pushed the plans for the Louvre's renovation forward.

PEI'S ENORMOUS SUBTERRANEAN ADDITION EFFECTIVELY MANAGES MOVEMENT AND PROVIDES NATURAL LIGHT WITHIN THE LOUVRE.

UNDER CONSTRUCTION, THE PYRAMID RISES IN THE CENTER OF NAPOLEON'S COURTYARD.

When the excavation began in the spring of 1985, Pei ordered the workers to build the main pyramid first and then dig out around it. Fearful that Mitterand's opponents would gain control in the upcoming elections and compromise his design, Pei wanted the appearance of a done deal despite the challenges it posed for construction. Pei's son Didi, an architect on the project, said, "It was a bit like building the roof before the house. Everyone was extremely nervous."

Throughout the project, the construction of the pyramid demanded much from Pei. He wanted the pyramid to be as light as the air around it. Commercial glass wasn't clear enough for Pei's exacting standards. Iron oxide gave it a greenish tint. The largest manufacturer of glass in France insisted that removing the iron oxide was impossible until a German company agreed to do it. Suddenly, French pride motivated the French manufacturer to agree to Pei's request.

The surface of glass contains tiny imperfections that dull its appearance. Pei ordered that the

ON MARCH 29, 1989, PRESIDENT FRANCOIS MITTERRAND CONGRATULATES I. M. PEI AT THE OPENING CEREMONY FOR THE LOUVRE'S PYRAMID ENTRANCE.

pyramid's nearly 800 diamond-shaped and triangular-shaped panes be polished to a crystal-like finish. Then, to minimize the appearance of the metal web that framed each pane, Pei called on a yacht maker to build a light, yet strong steel pyramidal form to hold the glass. When complete, the pyramid had to be bombproof, bulletproof, and strong enough to hold the heaviest of snowfalls. To keep the pyramid crystalline at all times, a team of rock climbers repel down the sheer glass sides armed with sponges and squeegees to clean away soot and pigeon droppings.

Despite all the attention paid to the pyramid, for Pei it was not the critical element of the design. He said, "The pyramid is not important. I'm sorry to say that. It's a symbol only. The most important piece of the work in the Louvre is the reorganization of the entire museum." However, Pei's pyramid did play a part in the reorganization, and Pei admits it had purpose in that respect. "What makes the pyramid important is not the form but the fact that it enables you to bring light to two levels below ground." Its position defining the center of the museum also serves the design. "It's a centralized entrance that enables you to go in the three surrounding wings of the Louvre, not one, because they're all interconnected." Pei had taken an awkward entrance with no visual appeal and transformed it into an elegant entry that handled large crowds efficiently.

With each passing day, week, month, year, the renovations of the Louvre grew on the people of France. One by one they were won over by the courtyard's beauty. Just as a century before, public opinion had turned from calling the Eiffel Tower "a pile of iron junk" to embracing it as the city's symbol, so had the pyramid ridden the tide from being vilified to championed. "I like to imagine that it is a French spirit that gives life to the fountains, to the pyramid, even if they were designed by an American," Pei wrote.

Never is the Louvre more beautiful than at night when hundreds of spotlights light Napoleon's courtyard. The seven computer-controlled fountains spout graceful floodlit pillars. And the pyramid—Pei's signature in the heart of Paris—gleams, with crystalline light. Now when Pei travels to Paris, he is recognized when he enters the courtyard. And the French, standing in line to enter the Louvre, break into applause.

FOUNTAINS SURROUND THE GLASS PYRAMID AS SEEN FROM THE LOUVRE'S ROOFTOP.

Miho Museum
Misono, Shigaraki, Shiga, Japan 1991-1997

Shortly after the grand opening of the Louvre, Pei celebrated his seventy-second birthday. Perhaps it was during that April in 1989 that Pei reflected on a birthday gift that his associates from Fragrant Hill had given him a decade earlier. The gift was a translation from the Lun-yü, which is a collection of Confucian sayings that describes the many stages of life. "At 15 I set my heart on learning; at 30 I firmly took my stand; at 40 I had no delusions; at 50 I knew the Mandate of Heaven; at 60 my ear was attuned; at 70 I followed my heart's desire without overstepping the boundaries of right." Now in his 70s, it was time for Pei to follow his heart's desire. Pei said, "I decided that I would no longer take on large projects, only some selected smaller ones."

Pei retired from I. M. Pei & Partners. His sons Didi and Sandi, who had risen within the company, struck out on their own, forming Pei Partnership Architects. Pei, free from the stresses and responsibilities of making payroll for a 300-person firm, could now step back and pursue the things that appealed to him. And sculpture was one of those things. Pei often said that if he had not become an architect, he would have loved to have been a sculptor.

Evidence for this admiration for sculpture can be traced all the way back to his first days as a practicing architect. Even when budget was a primary concern in the low-cost housing projects built with Zeckendorf, Pei found ways to include some form of sculpture in the design plans. So when Mihoko Koyama, heiress, art collector, and one of the richest women in Japan, approached Pei to build a bell tower in a secluded site 90 minutes southeast of Kyoto, Pei was eager to express himself using architecture as sculpture.

Koyama was then serving as head of a spiritual organization known as Shumei, where art and beauty are revered for their ability to nourish the soul and foster harmony among people everywhere. Shumei is not a religion but a philosophy of life. Its founder "believed that well-being is within everyone's reach through the spiritual exercise of Jyorei, an appreciation of art and beauty, and the care and reverence for our environment."

The bell tower was to stand on the grounds of the Shumei headquarters in Misono. Misono means "heavenly garden"—and heavenly it is. Here rolling pine-clad hilltops pitch into steep valleys. For centuries the Japanese have regarded these mountains as sacred land. By erecting a bell tower here, amid great natural beauty, the followers of Shumei hoped "that the harmonious sounds of these bells will carry peace and joy throughout the entire world."

To absorb the spirit of the site, Pei visited Misono. He noted its historical character when he approached the sanctuary by way of a path paved with cobblestones from Kyoto's old imperial city. In the soothing shade of wisteria and Japanese maples that lined the pathway, Pei contemplated the location's close connection to nature. The pathway curves as it approaches a cascading waterfall. It is customary for visitors to wash their hands and face in these waters before entering the sanctuary itself. Just beyond, the Great Plaza sprawls. This travertine expanse can hold 30,000 followers. And at the far end of this open plaza, a marble hall rises in the shape of Mount Fuji. The hall, which seats nearly 6,000 people, was designed by Minoru Yamasaki, the architect who also designed the twin towers of New York City's World Trade Center. All this, Pei took in while wandering the property.

In a flash of inspiration, which Pei described later as a near mystical impulse, the form of the bell tower took shape in his mind. He remembered an ivory bachi, or tool used to pluck a three-stringed musical instrument, that he'd picked up decades earlier in Kyoto because he admired its shape in a shop window. Later, the bachi had broken in storage. The break, Pei thought, had improved the sculptural interest of the bachi rather than damaging it. A bachi and a bell tower—how perfect, Pei thought. The two shared one mission—to deliver music.

Using the bachi as a model, Pei designed the nearly 200-foot bell tower to curve gently outward as it rose, to house 50 bells of varying sizes. Searching the globe for just the right materials, he chose white granite from Vermont to clad the exterior and had the bells cast in a bell foundry in the Netherlands.

Koyama, remembering an image of an angel playing the bachi in one of Kyoto's temples, christened the tower "The Joy of Angels." She was so delighted with Pei's execution of the bell tower that before it was even finished, she approached Pei to build a museum that would accomplish one of the three primary purposes of her spiritual practice—to foster appreciation of art by making it available to everyone.

Although Pei and Koyama did not speak the same language, they had developed a bond of mutual respect through their shared love of art, so it was hard for Pei to refuse her. However, Pei could not in good conscience build her museum on the site she first offered. It overlooked a parking lot, which would strip the museum of the sense of sanctuary—an element Pei perceived as critical for this structure. Convinced that he had lost the commission, he returned to New York only to be contacted shortly afterward. Koyama, rather than giving up Pei, had given up on the original site. She invited Pei to come see the new location.

The new site was not near a parking lot. In fact, it was not near anything—not even a road permitting access by motorized vehicle. It was so remote that Koyama and Pei's wife, Eileen, had to be carried up the steep slope in sedan chairs, while Pei struggled behind using a walking stick. But it was well worth the effort. Pei said that as he approached the proposed site, it brought back vivid childhood memories of a Chinese poem called "Peach Blossom Spring" by the fourth-century poet Tao Yuanming. This ancient poem tells the legend of a fisherman rowing a boat down a stream when suddenly he finds himself near a peach orchard. Scented peach petals float through the air, blanketing the stream and its banks in white petals. The enraptured fisherman leaves his boat to walk through the peach grove, where he discovers an opening in the mountain. Following the narrow winding path, he discovers utopia.

When Pei shared with Koyama how the site triggered the memory of "Peach Blossom Spring," he discovered that she too had read this poem as a child. They imagined that the approach to the museum should give the visitor the feeling of undertaking a journey like the fisherman's. This journey should create a sense of detachment from the real world, just as Yuanming's utopia had in the poem. Pei

INSPIRATION FOR THIS JAPANESE BELL TOWER, THE JOY OF ANGELS, IN MISONO CAME FROM A MUSICAL INSTRUMENT CALLED A BACHI.

I. M. PEI POINTS OUT FEATURES IN HIS MODEL OF THE PROPOSED MIHO MUSEUM TO HEIRESS AND PATRON TO THE MUSEUM, MIHOKO KOYAMA.

recalls, "This joint sharing of an idea enabled us to overcome the many difficulties." And many difficulties did follow, repeatedly testing their dedication to the project.

The first hurdle involved acquiring permits and permission. The site's location within a nature conservancy brought countless restrictions. Of course, it was those very restrictions that had protected the natural environment thus far. Koyama's daughter, Hiroko Koyama, took charge of navigating the sensitive byways of government rules and regulations, paving the way for Pei and his ambitious plans for the museum.

In addition to the requirements any builder would expect in a nature conservatory—rules that would preserve the landscape—there were many limits imposed on the building itself. One, the strict height restriction of 43 feet forced Pei to build 85 percent of the museum underground. This meant essentially removing the top of the mountain along with 7,000 trees growing there, and once construction was finished, bringing it all back again. Only an architect like I. M. Pei would think that moving a mountain was a "small select" retirement project.

Building underground also presented its own challenges. Earthquake tremors that travel underground could destroy the building. To prevent earthquake forces from damaging the museum walls, engineers suggested digging a trench around the building to act as a buffer.

Besides all the requirements and demands on the museum, by far the greatest trial was building a dramatic entrance. For that, Pei planned to tunnel through the adjacent mountain and span the valley in between with a 400-foot bridge. And as one had come to expect of Pei, the bridge itself was true sculptural design, contributing to the beauty of the project rather than detracting from it. The bridge's ninety-six supporting cables might have well been peach petals falling from the sky, for all their glory. Pei's structural engineer on the project, Leslie Robertson, said, "The bridge was a collaboration that brought out the best in both of us."

Once construction was underway, a new set of problems arose. Originally the plan was for the museum to house Koyama's collection of Japanese tea ceremony objects—a relatively modest number of works. But the new site, with its elaborate approach, demanded grander treasures. Koyama's daughter, Hiroko, shifted her energies from dealing with bureaucrats to dealing with art dealers around the world. Pei and the two Koyamas decided the focus of the collection would be objects connected to the Silk Road. Pei said, "I liked the idea, but I did not realize at what pace the museum design would have to be revised." This is where the underground aspect of the

THE SOUNDPROOF TUNNEL THROUGH THE MOUNTAIN ON THE APPROACH TO THE MIHO MUSEUM QUIETS THE MIND AND SIGNALS THE BEGINNING OF A JOURNEY AWAY FROM THE EVERYDAY WORLD.

THE GRACEFUL SUSPENSION BRIDGE OVER THE GORGE LEADS TO THE ENTRANCE OF THE MIHO MUSEUM. EIGHTY-FIVE PERCENT OF THE MUSEUM LIES UNDERGROUND. THE CONTOUR OF THE ORIGINAL MOUNTAIN REMAINS UNCHANGED.

design served him well. Pei said, "That was what saved us. We were able to expand to accommodate our needs."

One particularly tricky expansion involved hanging a rug. Not just any rug, but a 300-year-old Iranian carpet that the director of the Metropolitan Museum of Art in New York City had his eye on. After winning the bid, Koyama realized that the planned ceilings weren't high enough to hang it. The solution? Dig deeper.

In the end, the Koyamas put together a collection of 300 priceless objects acquired through major art dealers and museums all over the world which they displayed in two 11,000-square-foot wings that Pei added to the original design. The north wing showcases Japanese art, while the south wing exhibits works from the rest of Asia, Egypt, Greece, and Rome.

Of course Pei, being Pei, did not consider the project complete until the exterior was as thoughtfully arranged as the inside. And what would a Pei work be without at least one old, gnarled tree? At last he found the perfect 150-year-old pine tree in Tokyo. It now graces the entrance to the museum.

Just as with Fragrant Hill, Pei's primary concern was to meld tradition and modernity. Pei said, "I had the responsibility to respect the tradition that has developed through the centuries." And as in all of Pei's projects, geometry was the tool Pei used to express himself. "I believe in the triangle because it is the simplest and strongest geometric construct. You can create great spatial complexity through juxtaposition and combination. It is a lot like the music of Bach. . . . The music of Bach is a variation on a theme, and yet what richness he was able to give it! It continues to impress me and influence my architecture."

Pei denies he has a signature, but just as people know they are listening to Bach when they experience a particular variations of notes, we know when we are experiencing a Pei masterpiece. As we move through one of his creations, we come upon surprises that delight—and when we do, it's not hard to imagine Pei hiding in the wings, tickled by our enjoyment.

FROM INSIDE THE SILENT TUNNEL, VISITORS GET THEIR FIRST GLIMPSE OF THE ENTRANCE PAVILION'S TRADITIONAL CHINESE MOON-GATE DOORWAY.

MIHO MUSEUM

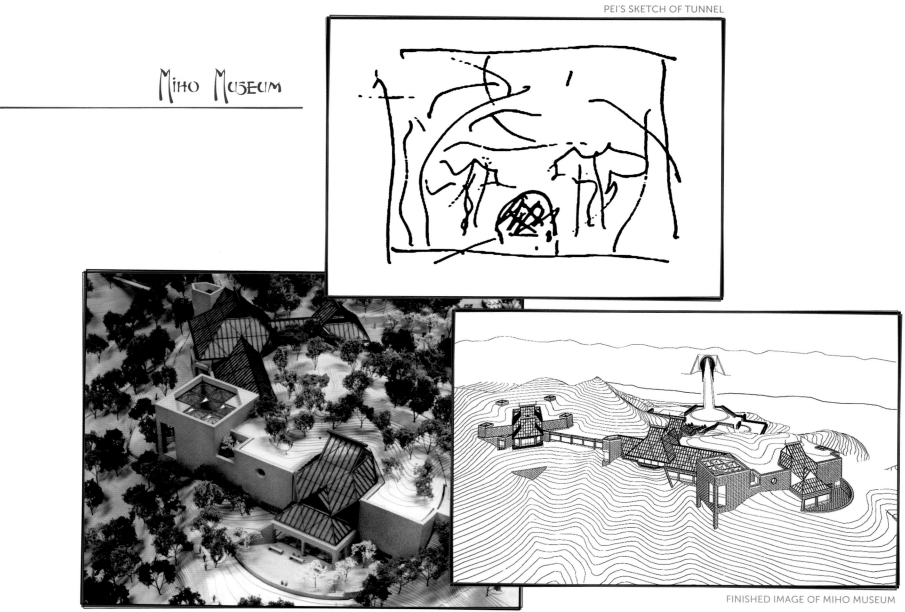

SITE MODEL DETAIL: SOUTH WING GALLERIES

FINISHED IMAGE OF MIHO MUSEUM

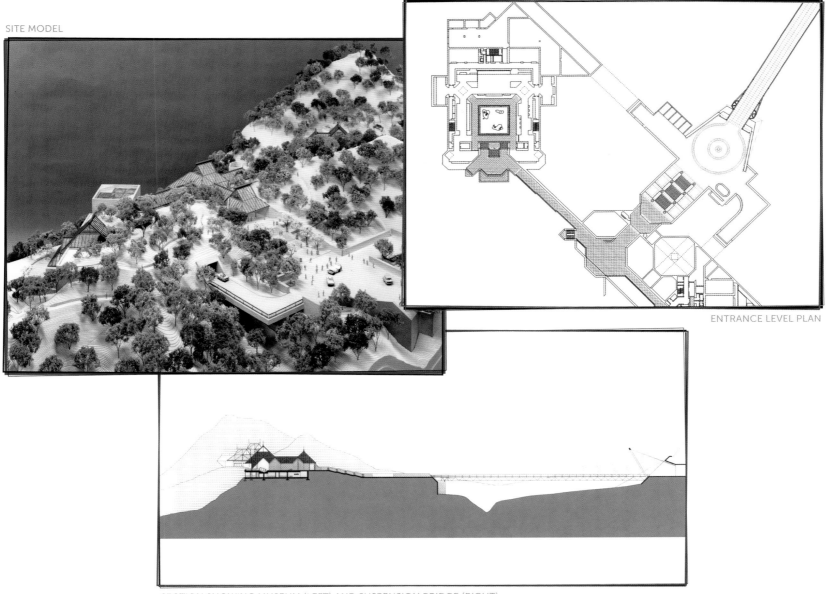

SITE MODEL

ENTRANCE LEVEL PLAN

SECTION SHOWING MUSEUM (LEFT) AND SUSPENSION BRIDGE (RIGHT)

89

Time, Place, and Purpose

Although most of Pei's career preceded the green movement, his designs incorporate many features attributed to environmentally responsible building. For instance, all of Pei's projects take advantage of natural light. The key purpose of the glass pyramids in the Louvre design was to flood the underground central hub with natural light. Through innovative design, Pei nearly halved the quantity of steel needed to construct the high-rise Bank of China in Hong Kong, conserving considerable natural resources. And in what might be considered a recycling achievement, when Pei addressed the planning commission to propose the NCAR building, he told them that in 5,000 years NCAR would be indistinguishable from the mountain.

Despite the fact that Pei's simplicity of design itself conserves natural resources, the purpose is not necessarily ecological. Pei said, "I belong to no group, nor do I engage myself in the architectural movements of the moment." Rather than imposing a particular stylistic choice on a project, the project dictates the design—not Pei the architect. Pei's job, as he sees it, is to discover the spirit of the place. Part of that discovery involves uncovering its history and honoring the past by infusing modern design with that historical essence. Pei explains that his approach "requires a full understanding of the three essential elements—time, place, purpose—to arrive at an ideal balance among them."

There is no finer example of Pei's personal challenge to discover the essence of the past and express that through modernism than the Museum of Islamic Art in Doha, Qatar. The city of Doha, on an island in the Persian Gulf, is known as "the city of balance" because of its ability to embrace the modern world without turning its back on tradition. It was here that Pei undertook one of his most difficult jobs. "It seemed to me that I had to grasp the essence of Islamic architecture. The difficulty of my task was that Islamic culture is so diverse, ranging from Iberia to Mughal India, to the gates of China and beyond."

Pei found his inspiration in Muslim fortresses and mosques centuries old. Pei's expression of time, place, and purpose in his design of the museum transcended a mere showcase for Islamic art. The museum's curator, Sabiha Al-Khemir, credits Pei with opening the very spirit of the objects on display for the public. She said, "Here is a museum in the Muslim world capable of bridging the gap between tradition and modernity. This is what I. M. Pei did

91

with the building. He actually reinterpreted Islamic architecture, giving it his own expression, one that is simultaneously personal and universal. In the manner that the building itself has created a bridge between tradition and modernity, so, too, the displays can embody the same link between the past and the present. . . ."

Although Pei claims that he does not have a stylistic signature, those who admire the austere beauty of his timeless designs, the seamless incorporation into their surroundings, and the vitality they bring to the people who use them, argue that a Pei building is instantly recognizable. Each project is testimony to his love of geometry, his passion for history, and his minimalist touch.

In 1983 Pei was honored with the prestigious Pritzker Architecture Prize. From the jury citation, we learn the depth and breadth of Pei's contribution that made him the clear choice for the Pritzker. "Ieoh Ming Pei has given this century some of its most beautiful interior spaces and exterior forms. Yet the significance of his work goes far beyond that. His concern has always been the surroundings in which his buildings rise. He has refused to limit himself to a narrow range of architectural problems. His work over the past forty years includes not only palaces of industry, government and culture, but also moderate and low-income housing. His versatility and skill in the use of materials approach the level of poetry."

Never satisfied to rest on past accomplishments, Pei continues into his ninth decade to push the boundaries of technology and design. With a boyish eagerness that belies his years, Pei embraces a new century and all that comes with it. The words he chose to close his acceptance speech for the Pritzker Prize illuminate the way of thinking that made Pei a visionary. "Let us all be attentive to new ideas, to advancing means, to dawning needs, to impetuses of change so that we may achieve, beyond architectural originality, a harmony of spirit in the service of man."

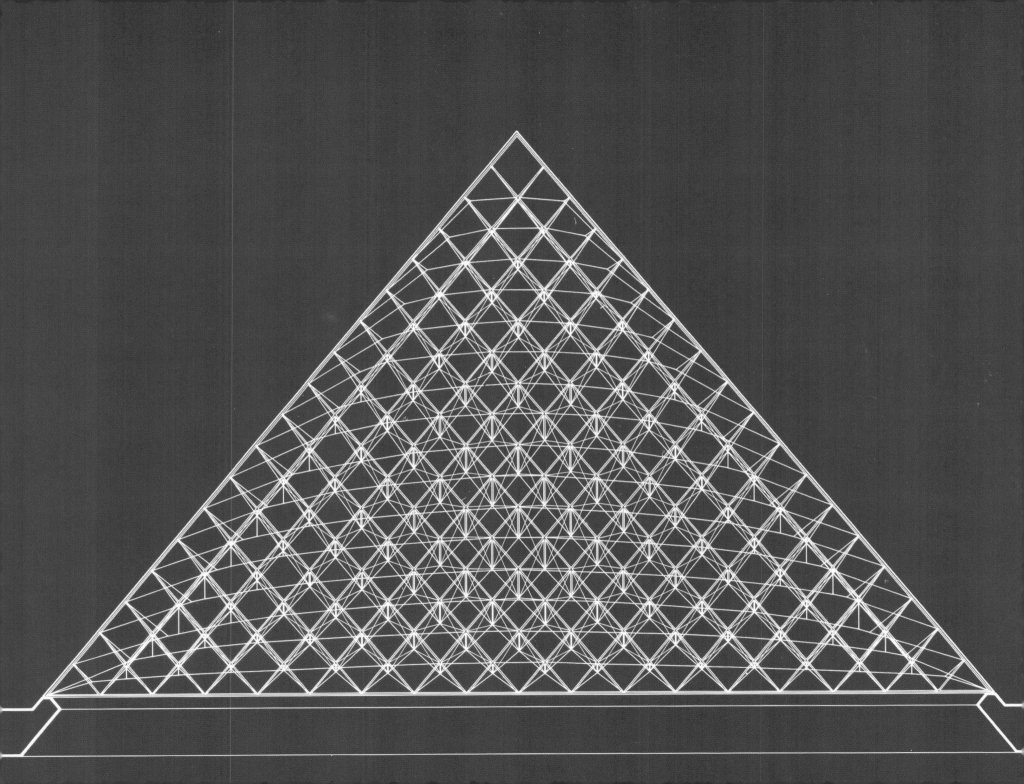

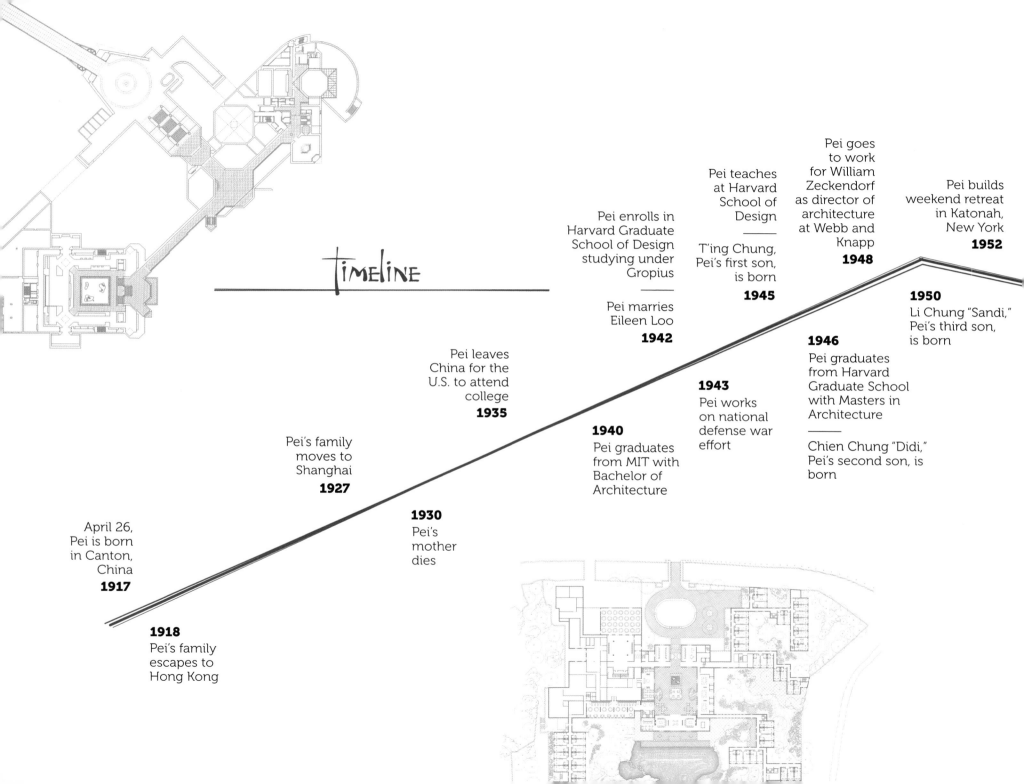

Timeline

1917
April 26,
Pei is born
in Canton,
China

1918
Pei's family
escapes to
Hong Kong

1927
Pei's family
moves to
Shanghai

1930
Pei's
mother
dies

1935
Pei leaves
China for the
U.S. to attend
college

1940
Pei graduates
from MIT with
Bachelor of
Architecture

1942
Pei marries
Eileen Loo

Pei enrolls in
Harvard Graduate
School of Design
studying under
Gropius

1943
Pei works
on national
defense war
effort

Pei teaches
at Harvard
School of
Design
———
T'ing Chung,
Pei's first son,
is born
1945

1946
Pei graduates
from Harvard
Graduate School
with Masters in
Architecture
———
Chien Chung "Didi,"
Pei's second son, is
born

Pei goes
to work
for William
Zeckendorf
as director of
architecture
at Webb and
Knapp
1948

1950
Li Chung "Sandi,"
Pei's third son,
is born

Pei builds
weekend retreat
in Katonah,
New York
1952

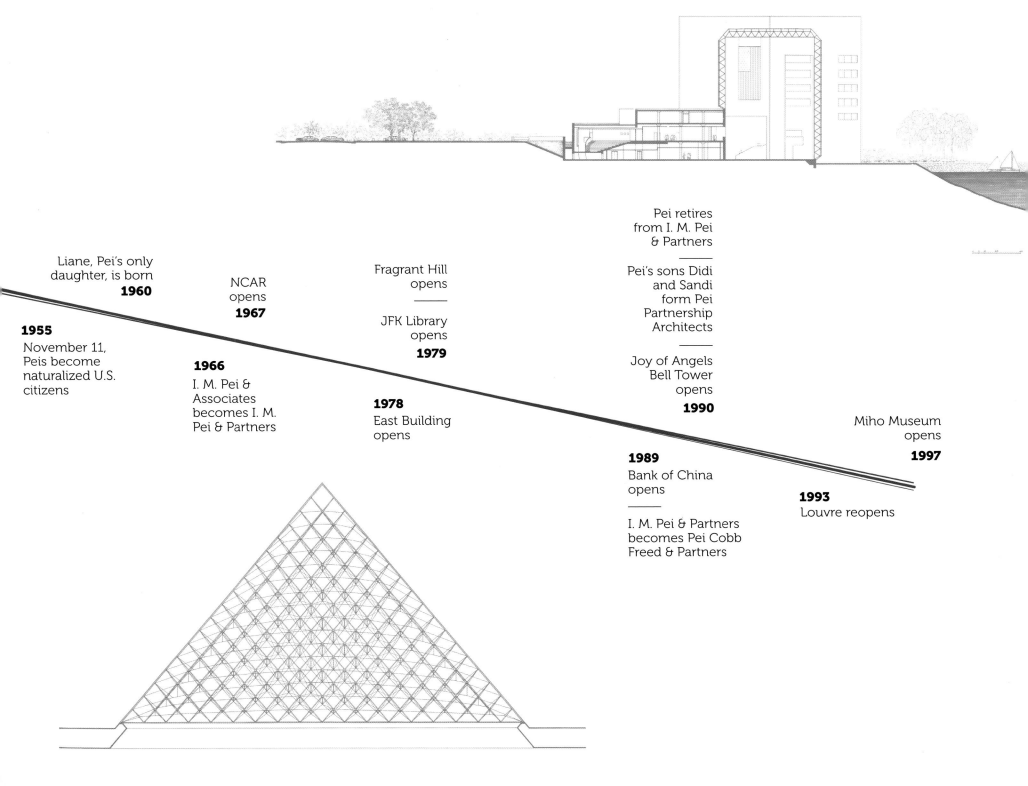

1955
November 11, Peis become naturalized U.S. citizens

Liane, Pei's only daughter, is born
1960

NCAR opens
1967

1966
I. M. Pei & Associates becomes I. M. Pei & Partners

Fragrant Hill opens
———
JFK Library opens
1979

1978
East Building opens

Pei retires from I. M. Pei & Partners

Pei's sons Didi and Sandi form Pei Partnership Architects
———
Joy of Angels Bell Tower opens
1990

1989
Bank of China opens
———
I. M. Pei & Partners becomes Pei Cobb Freed & Partners

1993
Louvre reopens

Miho Museum opens
1997

Bibliography

Blake, Peter. *No Place Like Utopia: Modern Architecture and the Company We Kept*. New York: Alfred A. Knopf, 1993.

Boehm, Gero Von. *Conversations with I. M. Pei: Light Is the Key*. New York: Prestel, 2000.

Cannell, Michael. *I. M. Pei: Mandarin of Modernism*. New York: Carol Southern Books, 1995.

Englar, Mary. *I. M. Pei*. Chicago: Heinemann Raintree, 2005.

Gutman, Robert. *Architectural Practice: A Critical View*. Princeton, NJ: Princeton Architectural Press, 1988.

I. M. Pei & Partners. *I. M. Pei & Partners Drawings for the East Building, National Gallery of Art: Its Evolution in Sketches, Renderings, and Models, 1968-1978: an exhibition*. Developed by Adams Davidson Galleries with the cooperation of the National Gallery of Art and the American Institute of Architects Foundation. Washington D.C., 1978.

Jencks, Charles. *The New Paradigm in Architecture: The Language of Post-Modern Architecture*. New Haven: Yale University Press, 2002.

Jodidio, Philip, and Janet Adams Strong. *I. M. Pei: Complete Works*. New York: Rizzoli, 2008.

Jones, E. Michael. *Living Machines: Bauhaus Architecture as Sexual Ideology*. San Francisco: Ignatius Press, 1995.

Levy, Matthys, and Mario Salvadori. *Why Buildings Fall Down: How Structures Fail*. New York: W. W. Norton & Company, 2002.

Lukinson, Sara. *First Person Singular, I. M. Pei* (video recording). Produced and directed by Peter Rosen for Lives and Legacy Films. PBS Home Video. Alexandria, VA, 1997.

Lukinson, Sara. *I. M. Pei; The Museum on the Mountain Miho Museum*, Shiga, Japan (video recording). Produced by Peter Rosen and Tim Culbert. Directed by Peter Rosen. Home Vision Entertainment. United States, 2003.

Miller, Naomi and Keith Morgan. *Boston Architecture: 1975-1990*. New York: Prestel, 1990.

Plunz, Richard. *A History of Housing in New York City: Dwelling Type and Social Change in the American Metropolis*. New York: Columbia University Press, 1990.

Rauterburg, Hanno. *Talking Architecture: Interviews with Architects*. New York: Prestel, 2008.

Reid, Aileen. *I. M. Pei*. Avenel, New Jersey: Crescent Books, 1995.

Wells, Matthew. *30 Bridges*. New York: Watson-Guptill Publications, 2002.

Wiseman, Carter. *I. M. Pei: A Profile in American Architecture*. New York: Harry N. Abrams, Inc., 2001.

Zeckendorf, William, and Edward McCreary. *The Autobiography of William Zeckendorf*. New York: Holt, Rinehart and Winston, 1970.

Notes

THE EARLY YEARS

"It was a very exciting, but": Boehm, p. 21.

"pat a son on the back, or": Wiseman, p. 31.

"Then, just before dawn": Cannell, p. 50.

"This building was going up": Boehm, p. 22.

"You see a bit": Wiseman, p. 189.

"Their shapes have hopefully been": Cannell, p. 58.

PEI COMES TO THE UNITED STATES

"I was not satisfied with the Beaux-Arts training": Cannell, p. 68.

"Le Corbusier's three books were my bible": Boehm, p. 36.

"the street has been killed": http://www.kirjasto.sci.fi/lecorbu.htm

"I take great pleasure in making large": http://www.princeton.edu/pr/news/01/q1/0131-artmus.htm

"He was insolent. He was" and "were probably the most important days": Cannell, p. 69.

"It was awful": Cannell, p. 76

"If the college is to be the cultural breeding": Jones, p. 78.

"I wouldn't say he was a great": http://www.bbc.co.uk/radio3/johntusainterview/pei_transcript.shtml

"I wanted to go home": Cannell, p. 86.

HOUSE ARCHITECT

"The whole environment was seedy": Wiseman, p. 47.

"I wanted to learn something": Boehm, p. 49.

"What was important was creating": Boehm, p. 51.

"Feelings of sorrow at having": Cannell, p.155.

"America has been a blessing": Cannell, p. 156.

"They will cheapen the building": Cannell, p. 126.

"He was very open minded": http://www.bbc.co.uk/radio3/johntusainterview/pei_transcript.shtml

"He needed eight hours of sleep": Wiseman, p. 50.

"I had very little money in those": Jodidio, p. 33.

"This was not a showpiece": Jodidio, p. 33.

"I was doing a lot of low cost": http://www.bbc.co.uk/radio3/johntusainterview/pei_transcript.shtml

"I knew that if I stayed": Wiseman, p. 69.

"In a way, Zeckendorf's financial": Cannell, p. 136.

NATIONAL CENTER FOR ATMOSPHERIC RESEARCH

"Walter Roberts was a very": http://www.bbc.co.uk/radio3/johntusainterview/pei_transcript.shtml

"There in the Colorado mountains": Boehm, p. 60.

"The site is, indeed": http://www.ucar.edu/communications/ucar25/experiment.html

"Here it is": Wiseman, p. 78.

"I acquired an appetite": Cannell, p. 161.

JOHN F. KENNEDY PRESIDENTIAL LIBRARY

"I had to think about the president": http://www.jfklibrary.org/Research/The-Ernest-Hemingway-Collection/~/media/assets/Foundation/newsletter/2005_winterspring.pdf

"He was so full of promise":

http://www.jfklibrary.org/NR/rdonlyres/1F619588-997E-4BD0-A41B-0F6D9FDBE579/796/forum_pei.html

"When we excavated":

http://www.jfklibrary.org/NR/rdonlyres/1F619588-997E-4BD0-A41B-0F6D9FDBE579/796/forum_pei.html

"People coming from the exhibition": Jodidio, p. 108.

"I lost my spirit": Jodidio, p. 107.

NATIONAL GALLERY OF ART, EAST BUILDING

"This is probably the most": Cannell, p. 245.

"Otherwise they will spend five": Cannell, p. 249.

"When I have to find": Cannell, p. 246.

"Can you build it?": Cannell, p. 256.

"What had seemed so dazzlingly": Cannell, p. 263.

"Not the least of these great masters": Cannell, p. 272.

FRAGRANT HILL HOTEL

"I just couldn't do it": Cannell, p. 304.

"At the time, everybody": Cannell, p. 303.

"They were horrified": Cannell, p. 303.

"I didn't even hesitate": Cannell, p. 304.

"Chinese architects...couldn't": Cannell, p. 305.

"Architecture has to come": Cannell, pp. 305-306.

"A Chinese garden is like": Jodidio, p. 182.

"In the West, a window": Cannell, p. 306.

"China is a country with a long": Jodidio, p. 182.

"one of the most difficult experiences": Jodidio, p. 184.

"There was blood everywhere": Cannell, p. 313.

"It stunk to high heaven": Cannell, p. 317.

"I was so tired at one point": Wiseman, p. 205.

"It looks Chinese": translated from Chinese, Cannell, p. 322.

"They are not doing the wrong": Wiseman, p. 206.

"I. M.'s legacy": Wiseman, p. 206.

"This more than anything": Jodidio, p. 181.

BANK OF CHINA

"This is Chinese, very respectful": Cannell, p. 327.

"When the lease runs out": Wiseman, p. 288.

"After the budget was set": Jodidio, p. 195.

"If a building is not properly sited": Jodidio, p. 196.

"My father has a way of working": Cannell, p. 332.

"It was like watching the whole": Wiseman, p. 289.

"It represented a new way of building": Cannell, p. 333.

"If you only have so much money": Jodidio, p. 196.

"It's almost like a giant drop of glue": Jodidio, p. 198.

"It is in the union of technology": Jodidio, p. 200.

"Feng shui masters are like lawyers": Pei address, Committee of One Hundred, Los Angeles, Feb. 25, 1995.

"It hurt me very deeply": Pei address, Asia Society, New York, September, 24, 1991.

"As I worked with a new generation of Chinese:" *New York Times*, June 22, 1989.
http://news.google.com/newspapers?nid=1948&dat=19890623&id=WuIjAAAAIBAJ&sjid=MNYFAAAAIBAJ&pg=1094,1441776\

LOUVRE

"If it was to continue as a museum": Wiseman, p. 233.

"I wanted someone capable": Wiseman, p. 232.

"Pei was on every list": Wiseman, p. 233.

"I'd already decided": Cannell, p. 7.

"had been right 4,000 years ago": Wiseman, p. 238.

"mind-boggling, shells were landing": Wiseman, p. 258.

"It was a bit like building": Cannell, p.25.

"The pyramid is not important": http://www.bbc.co.uk/radio3/johntusainterview/pei_transcript.shtml

"What makes the pyramid important": Jodidio, p. 240.

"I like to imagine that it is a French": Jodidio, p. 243.

MIHO MUSEUM

"At 15 I set my heart on learning": http://factsanddetails.com/china.php?itemid=90&catid=3 and http://www.religionfacts.com/a-z-religion-index/confucianism.htm

"I decided that I would no longer": Boehm, p. 97.

"believed that wellbeing is within": http://www.shumei.org/artandbeauty/misono_tour.html

"that the harmonious sounds": http://www.shumei.org/artandbeauty/misono_tour.html

"This joint sharing of an idea": Boehm, p. 100.

"The bridge was a collaboration": Wiseman, p. 319.

"I liked the idea, but": Jodidio, p. 266.

"That was what saved us": Jodidio, p. 266.

"I had the responsibility to": Boehm, p. 99.

"I believe in the triangle": Boehm, pp. 101-102.

TIME PLACE AND PURPOSE

"I belong to no group, nor do": Boehm, p. 112.

"requires a full understanding": Boehm, p. 113.

"It seemed to me that I had to": Jodidio, p. 329.

"Here is a museum in the Muslim": Jodidio, p. 337.

"Ieoh Ming Pei has given this century": http://www.pritzkerprize.com/laureates/1983/jury.html

"Let us all be attentive to new ideas":

http://www.pritzkerprize.com/laureates/1983/ceremony_speech1.html

Further Exploration

SUGGESTED READING

Enlgar, Mary. *I.M. Pei: Asian-American Biographies.* Chicago: Heinemann Raintree, 2006.

Hollihan-Elliot, Shiela. *Art and Architecture in China: The History and Culture of China.* Broomall, PA: Mason Crest Publishers, 2005.

Macaulay, David. *Great Moments in Architecture.* Boston: Houghton Mifflin, 1978.

Oxlade, Chris. *Skyscrapers: Uncovering Technology.* Richmond Hills, Ontario: Firefly Books, 2006.

Pease, Pamela. *Design Dossier: Architecture.* Chapel Hill: Paintbox Press, 2010.

Salvadori, Mario. *The Art of Construction: Projects and Principles for Beginning Engineers & Architects.* Chicago: Chicago Review Press, 2000.

Salvadori, Mario. *Why Buildings Stand Up: The Strength of Architecture.* New York: W.W Norton & Co., 2002.

WEBSITES

Chinese Rock Gardening
http://www.metmuseum.org/TOAH/hd/cgrk/hd_cgrk.htm

Fragrant Hill Hotel
http://www.pcfandp.com/a/p/7905/s.html

John F. Kennedy Library
http://www.pcfandp.com/a/p/7617/s.html

presidential library home page
http://www.jfklibrary.org/

The Lion Grove Garden, Suzhou, China
http://www.suzhou.gov.cn/english/Travel/10.shtml

Louvre
http://www.pcfandp.com/a/p/8315/s.html

Louvre home page
http://www.louvre.fr/llv/commun/home.jsp?bmLocale=en

Miho Museum
http://www.miho.or.jp/english/collect/collect.htm

National Gallery of Art, East Wing
http://www.pcfandp.com/a/p/6810/s.html

National Gallery of Art home page
http://www.nga.gov/

NCAR
http://www.pcfandp.com/a/p/6146/s.html

NCAR home page
http://www.ncar.ucar.edu/

Peach Blossom Spring by Tao Qian
http://afe.easia.columbia.edu/ps/china/taoqian_peachblossom.pdf

YouTube video of "The Tale of Peach Blossom Spring": http://www.youtube.com/watch?v=8vQFm1iPU0Y

Pei Designs

**Bank of America Tower at International Place
(formerly Miami World Trade Center,
originally CenTrust Tower)**
Miami, Florida
completed 1986

Bank of China Tower
Hong Kong, China
completed 1989

Bedford-Stuyvesant Superblock
Brooklyn, New York
completed 1969

**Cecil and Ida Green Center for Earth Sciences,
Massachusetts Institute of Technology**
Cambridge, Massachusetts
completed 1964

Cleo Rogers Memorial County Library
Columbus, Indiana
completed 1969

Court House Square
Denver, Colorado
completed 1960

Creative Artists Agency
Beverly Hills, California
completed 1989

Dallas City Hall
Dallas, Texas
completed 1977

Des Moines Art Center Addition
Des Moines, Iowa
completed 1968

Everson Museum of Art
Syracuse, New York
completed 1968

FAA Air Traffic Control Towers (50)
various cities, United States and abroad
completed 1965

Four Seasons Hotel
New York, New York
completed 1993

Fragrant Hill Hotel
Beijing, China
completed 1982

Grand Louvre
Paris, France
phase I completed 1989
Grand Louvre
phase II completed 1993
Paris, France

Guggenheim Pavilion,
The Mount Sinai Medical Center Expansion
and Modernization
New York, New York
completed 1992

Herbert F. Johnson Museum of Art,
Cornell University
Ithaca, New York
completed 1973

IBM Headquarters, Entrance Pavilion and Site Enhancement
Armonk, New York
completed 1985

Indiana University Art Museum and Academic Building
Bloomington, Indiana
completed 1982

John Fitzgerald Kennedy Library
Boston, Massachusetts
completed 1979
extension completed 1991

JPMorgan Chase Tower, United Energy Plaza
Houston, Texas
completed 1982

Kips Bay Plaza
New York, New York
completed 1963

Kirklin Clinic
University of Alabama Health Services Foundation
Birmingham, Alabama
completed 1992

**Laura Spelman Rockefeller Halls,
Princeton University**
Princeton, New Jersey
completed 1974

Luce Memorial Chapel
Taichung, Taiwan
completed 1963

MasterCard International Global Headquarters
Purchase, New York
completed 1984

Mile High Center
Denver, Colorado
completed 1956

Morton H. Meyerson Symphony Center
Dallas, Texas
completed 1989

Museum of Fine Arts, West Wing and Renovation
Boston, Massachusetts
phase I completed 1981
phase II completed 1986

Museum of Islamic Art
Doha, Qatar
completed 2006

National Center for Atmospheric Research
Boulder, Colorado
completed 1967

National Gallery of Art, East Building
Washington, D.C.
completed 1978

Oversea-Chinese Banking Corporation Centre
Singapore
completed 1976

Paul Mellon Center for the Arts
The Choate School
Wallingford, Connecticut
completed 1973

Raffles City
Singapore
completed 1986

Rock and Roll Hall of Fame and Museum
Cleveland, Ohio
completed 1995

Rosemary Hall Science Center
The Choate School
Wallingford, Connecticut
completed 1989

Society Hill
Philadelphia, Pennsylvania
completed 1964

TWA Terminal Annex
JFK International Airport, New York, New York
completed 1970

University Plaza, New York University
New York, New York
completed 1967

Wiesner Building/Center for Arts & Media Technology, Massachusetts Institute of Technology
Cambridge, Massachusetts
completed 1984

WARDS

A few of the many honors I. M. Pei has received throughout his illustrious career:

2006 Erwin Wickert Foundation, Orient and Occident Prize

2003 National Building Museum, Henry C. Turner Prize for Innovation in Construction Technology

2003 Cooper-Hewitt, National Design Museum, Smithsonian Institution National Design Award, Lifetime Achievement Award

2001 The American Philosophical Society, the Thomas Jefferson Medal for distinguished achievement in the arts, humanities, or social sciences

1999 Historic Landmarks Preservation Center, New York Cultural Laureate

1998 The MacDowell Colony, Edward MacDowell Medal

1997 Brown University, Independent Award

1996 Municipal Art Society, New York City, Jacqueline Kennedy Onassis Medal

1994	New York State, Governor's Arts Award
1994	National Endowment for the Arts, Medal of Arts/Ambassador for the Arts Award
1994	Architectural Society of China (Beijing), Gold Medal for Outstanding Achievement in Architecture
1994	The Bezalel Academy of Arts and Design of Jerusalem, Jerusalem Prize for Arts and Letters
1993	United States, Medal of Freedom
1993	France, Officer of the Legion of Honor
1991	Colbert Foundation, First Award for Excellence
1990	University of California at Los Angeles, UCLA Gold Medal
1989	Japan, Praemium Imperiale for lifetime achievement in architecture
1988	United States, National Medal of Arts
1986	United States, the Medal of Liberty
1983	Hyatt Foundation, the Pritzker Architecture Prize
1981	National Arts Club, Gold Medal of Honor
1981	City of New York, Mayor's Award of Honor for Art and Culture
1981	France, Grand Medal of the Academy of Architecture
1979	Rhode Island School of Design, President's Fellow
1979	American Academy of Arts and Letters, Gold Medal for Architecture

1979	The American Institute of Architects, the Gold Medal
1978	American Society of Interior Designers, Elsie de Wolfe Award
1976	The Thomas Jefferson Memorial, Medal for Architecture
1973	The City Club of New York, for New York Award
1970	International Institute of Boston, Golden Door Award
1963	New York Chapter of the American Institute of Architects, Medal of Honor
1961	National Institute of Arts and Letters, Arnold Brunner Award

I. M. PEI ESCORTS HIS LOVELY WIFE EILEEN TO A FORMAL BENEFIT IN NEW YORK CITY.

Index

Page numbers in boldface are illustrations, tables, and charts.